Planning for Early Learning
Educating Young Children

Victoria Hurst taught history in secondary school and worked as a volunteer in an adult literacy programme before training for infant and nursery education. From 1979 to 1986 she taught in nursery education in inner London. She was a lecturer in early childhood education at Goldsmiths' College, University of London, and, as Research Fellow at Goldsmiths', is researching provision for early learning. She founded the Early Years Curriculum Group in 1989. She directed the *Quality in Diversity* curriculum development project of the Early Childhood Education Forum from 1994–6, and has been Deputy-Director of the *Principles into Practice* (1993–7) project which is investigating action-research strategies for professional development.

Planning for Early Learning
Educating Young Children

Second edition

Victoria Hurst

P·C·P

Paul Chapman
Publishing Ltd

Paul Chapman Publishing Ltd
144 Liverpool Road
London
N1 1LA

British Library Cataloguing in Publication Data

Hurst, Victoria
    Planning for early learning : educating young children. –
    2nd ed.
    1. Education, Preschool
    I. Title
    372.2'1

    ISBN 1 85396 344 5

Typeset by Dorwyn Ltd, Rowlands Castle, Hants
Printed and bound in Great Britain

A B C D E F G H   9 8 7

To the children, parents and colleagues
with whom these ideas were evolved
and in particular to the three children from whom I learned so much,
my daughters Charlotte and Miranda
and my nephew Inigo, who was born in 1971 and died in 1975

Acknowledgements

The education of young children is a collaborative and social business. Early childhood practitioners also learn with and from each other in much the same way. I have been inspired, challenged and comforted by my colleagues at Goldsmiths', in the Early Years Curriculum Group, in the *Principles into Practice* project, in the *Quality in Diversity* project and the Early Childhood Education Forum, and in all the settings I have been fortunate enough to work in.

While writing the first edition of this book I was fortunate to have the stimulus and companionship of Margaret Edgington, formerly known as Margaret Lally – without this it would have been a much less rewarding experience!

My husband's interest and support have been invaluable, as always.

Victoria Hurst
London, March 1997

Contents

Preface to the Second Edition

This book is addressed to the practitioners who carry the responsibility for young children's education and welfare in educational settings. Since the first edition of this book there have been many changes, some social and some political in origin, and some which are changes in understanding about young children. The task of the early childhood practitioner has become more complex and more challenging as a result.

There has been an increase in demand for day care for babies and children under three. In the past, it was assumed that 'education' was something that could be left until after three, but research into brain development (Carnegie Corporation, 1994) has brought to light the fact that poor provision for learning at this early stage can permanently damage the brain.

Nursery vouchers have completed the trend of early admission to infant school. Over 80 per cent of four-year-olds are now in infant school classrooms. These classrooms are rarely the equal of local authority nursery education provision in staffing, staff qualifications, accommodation, resourcing or curriculum. They are also in striking contrast with voluntary and private provision in terms of staff ratios.

As the National Curriculum for five- to seven-year-olds is 'bedded down' and the Desirable Outcomes for four-year-olds are introduced to support it, 'baseline' assessment at five is being brought in to balance National Curriculum assessment at seven. Settings must carry out these responsibilities, yet practitioners are aware that they must also provide for young children's different starting points, their differences in development, home background, special needs and preschool experience.

Practitioners in all sectors are eager to improve their practice and develop better approaches to the curriculum, as is shown by the *Quality in Diversity* project (Early Childhood Education Forum, draft papers, 1997). Yet many practitioners working with the under-eights are not specifically trained for the age-group they are working with, and others have not updated their initial qualifications (Blenkin, *et al.* 1995). Few can afford the time and money needed to undertake further training; can new findings from research and development projects help to improve their practice and deepen their understanding through their daily work?

The answers to these questions are to be found in the early years curriculum and in the findings of recent research and development projects. They are not answers for practitioners alone, although practitioners have to take the lead in proclaiming their implications. If we are to plan appropriately for early learning we must see it as a responsibility shared between parents, practitioners, providers and professional organizations; all play a part in decisions that affect children. I hope that this book may help early years practitioners to articulate the needs of young children more effectively and gain widespread support for realistic measures to improve their educational opportunities. By far the most promising avenue is through the increasing expertise and articulacy of early childhood practitioners, and their growing consensus across all the sectors and across the age-phases from birth to eight years old. I hope that this book will help with these important developments in the field of early childhood education.

Introduction

This book describes both the need for greater understanding of young children's capacities and potential, and the need for practical tools with which to describe and develop good practice in the provision of education for children in the crucial early years of education. The focus of the book is on the early years of education, which are internationally understood to include all the years of greatest emotional and physical dependence from birth to eight. The approaches put forward here suggest ways of educating children up to the age of eight in any setting, drawing on insights about development and learning at this early stage. The emphasis is on children's involvement in learning, and what practitioners can do to enhance this. This book sets out how practitioners can structure and organize their thinking about early education and the curriculum so that they support and extend children's learning and development; it goes on to show how, through observing and analysing children's responses to what they provide, practitioners can judge the effectiveness of their educational provision and learn more about the education of young children.

Improving educational achievement

If we are to improve educational achievement we need to have a better understanding of the education of our youngest children, and a greater expertise in our provision for early learning. Access to early education, and benefit from this access, depend to a large extent on the practitioner's understanding and skill in providing a curriculum that is appropriate for all the individual children in the setting. Children's particular learning strategies, experiences and needs, including special educational needs, should determine the way the curriculum is structured and implemented. Similarly, children's home experiences, their relationships with parents, siblings,

wider family and friends, their languages and the family and community cultural setting, are the material through which they learn,
and should be reflected in the curriculum and the way opportunities for learning are provided. This is essential for equal opportunity of access to education, but it is very demanding and it makes
early education a complex specialism, in which a high degree of
professional expertise is necessary. The combination of child
development knowledge, subject curriculum knowledge and the
practical ability to bring this knowledge together meaningfully for
a particular group of young children is a demanding task. Moreover, success in this task is also dependent on interpersonal sensitivity and skill in providing the social basis for learning, which
should be developed in partnership with children's families.

It is the aim of this book to illuminate the task of the early years
educator through examples drawn from educational settings, and
to offer some practical strategies for tackling different aspects of
this task.

Practitioners' contexts: changes since 1991

The context in which practitioners carry out their task must also be
considered. In the years since the first edition (1991), some things
have not changed. Early years practitioners as a whole are still
underfunded, poorly resourced and their training and further
qualifications are inadequately provided for; see, for instance, the
report of the findings of the *Principles into Practice* project (Blenkin
et al., 1995). They still work in a great diversity of settings, which
has both advantages and disadvantages, as the *Quality in Diversity*
project has shown (see Chapter 1).

However, some significant changes have taken place in the years
since the first edition; much has happened to highlight early learning, and while this in itself is cause for satisfaction, there is also
cause for concern that the effects of this highlighting may lead to
serious unforeseen problems.

Children under three used to be omitted from discussions of
educational standards because it was assumed by policy-makers
that they were cared for at home, or that their carers and practitioners were not concerned with 'teaching' them. Practitioners
working with babies and children under three have instead been
guided by the regulations of the Children Act, 1989 and have benefited from the high priority it gives to quality of provision for

learning and to the role and culture of families. However, the separation of education and care standards is unhelpful, and has undermined the educational role of practitioners in 'non-educational' settings. The growing number of young mothers in employment makes it vital that any proposed criteria for quality in early education include the under-threes. At present, the Children Act remains the only statutory regulation and guidance for the rapidly growing voluntary and private sector. The childminders, private and workplace nurseries, community nurseries, crèches and playgroups that provide for increasing numbers of babies, toddlers and two-year-olds are thrown onto their own resources for professional development and in-service training, with variable amounts of help from local authority social services and education departments. If children are to have the educational experiences they need, we must take on board the needs of their practitioners for support in working out how to provide for them in the face of policies that are not based on understanding of their learning needs.

The introduction of nursery vouchers in 1996, controversial though it was, certainly demonstrated central government's commitment to each parent's right to have access to pre-compulsory education. However, what is missing from the new regard for early education is an understanding that emphasizes its role in children's development, in their capacities as social and moral beings and in their lifelong attitudes to learning. The striking increase in concern about older children's attitudes and behaviour during the 1990s shows that there is a demand for education that supports social, emotional and moral development, yet there is little understanding of what this education should be like in the early years. This is largely because the nature and potential of very young children tend to be underestimated, and instruction is given where in fact children would benefit more from being reasoned with as moral beings who are capable of taking responsibility for themselves.

Education in the early years is seen here as being concerned with making links between learning at home and in the setting. Chapter 7 focuses on working in collaboration with parents, but every chapter builds on the idea that home learning is the starting point for each child. Much has been written about how to work in partnership with parents in early childhood, and the Children Act's priority for family culture has permeated much of recent literature.

This shows understanding of the formative influence of home and family, and how emphasis on the need for respect for children's home languages and culture has increased. Parental confidence is a theme that emerges as important, too, as in Pugh and De'Ath, 1996 and in Pugh *et al.*, 1994, and this leads to a curriculum issue. There is a conflict between the characteristic early years principle of education that reflects children's earliest learning with their families and communities and the demand for nationally-comparable standards of achievement at the ages of five and seven. The energy and expertise that bilingual learners generate can be better capitalized on if the curriculum can reflect their achievements, for instance, and this affects the whole group of children. Children with special needs, and there are many in the early years, particularly need provision for learning that builds on their home achievements. It is not just a question of conflict between the individual child's home culture and the culture of formal education; it is a conflict between individual achievement and formal accountability. Early years practitioners need to work much more closely with parents to develop continuous assessment that does justice to children's achievements and provides useful evidence for the next steps in provision for their learning.

There are important curriculum issues here, which provide links to the other main themes of the book. How to make provision for learning reflect home learning is as important a question as how to make it playful, and in many respects the two aims are united (see p. 59). Challenging questions arise from reviewing what is known about the personalized and playful ways in which children under eight learn; practitioners in infant education have been rightly concerned about the conflict between children's needs for a curriculum that is directly linked to their existing understanding and the requirement to produce a standardized level of performance at the age of seven for purposes of accountability.

The development of appropriate standards in early education has been held back by lack of understanding about developmental approaches to education and how they underpin the learning of subject-based knowledge. This 'missing step' in the concept of early education must be repaired; without it, young children's learning tends to be restricted by the top-down version of the curriculum enshrined in the National Curriculum structure which was introduced by the Education Reform Act in 1988. The breadth, depth and intellectual rigour of learning that can be achieved when practitioners work closely with children is described, and this is explained in terms of children's learning and development through their home experiences and through play.

Now that central government has imposed its own definition of the preschool curriculum in the *Desirable Outcomes for Children's Learning on Entering Compulsory Education* (School Curriculum and Assessment Authority, 1996) and its own model of assessment on entry to compulsory schooling (SCAA, 1997), those who teach the three- to five-year-olds will have concerns about how to develop curriculum plans that meet these requirements in a way that enhances children's learning. Both of these innovations show that pre-compulsory education is valued only as preparation for the subjects of the National Curriculum rather than as an end in itself. This, and how the balance can be redressed, will be discussed in the context of ideas about the curriculum in the early years from birth to eight, and the influential role of the under-fives curriculum within the early years curriculum.

Underestimation of young children's abilities in all spheres is common, and it is particularly likely to happen now that almost all four-year-olds in England and Wales are in infant school reception classes. This rapid change, which has taken place since the mid-1980s, means that children who could have previously been the oldest and most responsible ones in an appropriate preschool setting, leading younger children in learning in indoor and outdoor environments planned for their education, are now in infant classrooms where they rarely have the planned outdoor learning, staffing, accommodation, resources and curriculum which would enable them to be independent learners. As a result, they become more dependent on adults to motivate them and to meet their needs, just when lower staffing levels mean that they need to be more independent. Those who teach in reception or 'early admission' classes are under great pressure, and this works against their being able to draw back and reflect on how to improve what they do for their children. Governors and headteachers should make a policy of visiting maintained nursery education settings and comparing the experiences of children and adults with what is available in early admission and reception classes; reception classes have a long way to go before they can claim to offer four-year-olds anything approaching the educational opportunities they have a right to. Senior management should also consider changes in expectations and curriculum which could free children from dependence and free staff from the incessant demands of very young children who do not have enough space, equipment, outdoor playspace and adult leadership to be independent learners. Within the same primary school, it is possible to find nursery children using scissors, sellotape, staplers, paste, glue sticks, pens and pencils by themselves, and carpentry equipment, garden spades and climbing apparatus with adult supervision, while slightly older children in the reception class need adult help with writing and drawing equipment, and do not have access to carpentry equipment or a planned outdoor learning environment. In one school, a support teacher asked whether reception and year 1 children's parents should not be asked to teach them how to use scissors and how to hold a pen in order to make the work of their teachers less burdensome; the nursery teacher commented that all the nursery children could do this and more quite independently. Somehow, the conditions in reception classes, which may be accepted as normal or inevitable by primary staff but are usually very different from nursery education standards, are teaching the children to be dependent, and consequently undermining the expertise of reception teachers.

The risk of progressive deskilling of children in inappropriate classrooms places a grave responsibility on staff and governing bodies to take care that early admission promotes rather than hinders children's full development and learning. What can be done about this will be discussed along with the central issues, problems and possibilities confronting early years practitioners today.

Practitioners themselves have been trying since early in the 1990s to take a leading role in the definition of standards for the care and education of the under-eights. There have been some outstanding successes, particularly in the behind-the-scenes work of bodies such as the Early Childhood Education Forum, of which more in Chapter 1. However, the standards which practitioners seek to promote are dependent on having the appropriate tools for developing practice and demonstrating how certain approaches work better than others. The development of these tools is an essential step in the growth of the professionalism of early childhood educators. Observation has long been thought of as part of the process of creating an effective early years curriculum, but it can be even more than that; it can provide the evidence for professional evaluation of the curriculum and its implementation, and for judgements about educational developments. Observation, evaluation and professional judgements will be explored throughout this book, with a particular focus on the opportunities for practitioners' learning and self-development.

The role of nursery education

The early years curriculum or, more precisely, its remaining embodiment in the under-five or nursery curriculum, holds answers to some of the questions that arise from such issues as these. The argument of this book is that nursery education holds the key to improving educational achievement precisely because its model of the early years curriculum has not been so much affected by central government emphasis on 'traditional' methods and content in the way that the infant curriculum has. The nursery version of the early years curriculum still takes into account children's all-round development and the formation of their attitudes. Nursery education remains founded on the study of child development even as it takes on new ideas about the learning of subject disciplines. In particular, its fundamental understandings about learning and development are needed for the critical evaluation of proposals for education for children between birth and seven.

For instance, since the beginning of this century, nursery education has proclaimed the importance of outdoor play for children under five, yet, as the century ends, the trend is in the opposite direction; local authorities and schools continue to admit four-year-olds to reception classes where good provision for outdoor play is rarely available. The role of nursery education in setting standards for the education of all children under eight is an extremely important one; for instance, continuing concern about children's physical health should alert us to what we can learn from long-established nursery education provision for developing physical health and healthy habits and attitudes in the young. As long ago as 1918 H. A. L. Fisher introduced his Education Bill in the House of Commons under the theme of the 'Children's Charter'; he described it as a Bill 'that asserts the principle of the rights of youth'. One aspect of the provision intended was that nursery schools would be jointly funded through rates and taxes, and from these schools he expected a great improvement in physical health. 'The subject of nursery schools led the Minister to discuss the subject of provisions for physical education, on which he laid great stress' (Fisher, *The Times*, 14.3.97, 'On this day, March 14, 1918', p. 23).

The nursery curriculum, whose methods, content and philosophy have genuine and well-founded traditions that date back to the mid-nineteenth century at least and whose philosophy is even older, should be a source of insight into teaching and learning for all those who provide education for children in the under-three, preschool and infant stages. Its role is becoming increasingly important as pressure for formal achievement increases; it is good that recent research and development projects are addressing ways to increase and disseminate understanding of it. This book aims to contribute to the process by drawing attention to some of the knowledge and expertise nursery education has to offer, and showing how similar approaches can support and improve provision for learning across the age-phases in the years before eight.

1

Educating Young Children

The role of this chapter is to set out the essence of good practice in early years education as a framework for the rest of the book. The practical examples and quotations are introduced to illustrate what this should mean in terms of children's experience. All examples have their own limitations, and readers are invited to make similar reference to examples from their own experiences and reading in consultation with colleagues and parents.

The early years curriculum and development

The most important idea in early education is that it is not only to do with learning knowledge and skills but that it is a collaborative and developmental process. The mind is not like a shopping-basket, which is better filled if one shops at a more prestigious store, but like an active and growing force, which learns ways to learn in conjunction with other minds. Knowledge, understanding and skills are indeed acquired, but the teacher, the adult or more experienced learner, teaches through responding to the learner's manifest concerns and activities. This begins with the mothering response to even the youngest baby as she or he communicates interest by, say, an intense stare and cessation of sucking while feeding, or by following the adult's voice with head and body movements. The intuitive response of most adults who are in the mothering role with children at this age and stage is to engage with eyes and voice and touch; to meet the gaze, talk softly, hold more closely or pick the baby up, and then see what the baby does next. Childwatchers who, like Trevarthen (1993), have seen these exchanges as conversations have caught the social interaction that characterizes learning in early childhood.

This, I believe, should be the pattern from which all the sub-sequent educational responses to children develop, whether the adult is with her or his own child or is responsible for someone else's. In the case of another person's child, this means relating to what can be learned of the child's present interests and developmental levels of thinking and feeling; it also means considering his or her levels of physical and social functioning, because these affect how children learn. This approach to education requires the adult to be very well aware of the full range of learning activities and the understanding and knowledge suitable for children of this age and to be able to make flexible and sensitive provision from this knowledge-base as seems appropriate.

This search for the 'positive characteristics' of children's thinking builds on what they can do, and extends their achievements (Athey, 1990, pp. 16–18). Children themselves show us how best they can learn, and enable us to provide stimulating experiences for them. Observation of young babies shows how exciting and rewarding they find social experiences with adults, children and other babies (Goldschmied and Selleck, 1996; Trevarthen, 1996). Infants use their hands and mouths to explore objects, and need to have a variety selected to interest and extend them. Children in their second year of life use their mobility to choose and combine different play objects in ways that establish patterns. They need collections of objects to help them explore the making of rational choices to develop their cognitive capacities (Goldschmied and Jackson, 1994). Later on, children build on these early explorations and social experiences in their development of relationships, communication, exploration and investigation, representation and creativity and symbolic actions and thinking. What can we do to help children at their different stages?

The answer to this question lies in how we respond to what the children can do at present, and how we provide resources to enrich their experiences and challenge their thinking. It includes how the learning environment can be prepared so that children can use it for their own purposes, and the ways in which the initial provision can be developed according to children's responses. As an example, a visitor to a nursery for children of two and three would find much that was unexpected and that required discussion. He or she might note the following:

> Room set out with different areas for children to use, such as bricks, home corner etc. Things like puzzles and construction kits on tables, more in shelves for children to fetch if they want. Painting, drawing, cutting, sticking all ready to use. Outdoor playthings out already.

Children come in gradually and look for what they want to do. Parents talk to staff, go gradually after saying goodbye to children. Some organized time, like story and group activities, but mostly free for play etc. indoors and outdoors.

Questions might arise about the running of this group. 'How do staff know what children will want? How can they be certain that children are learning when they don't directly teach them? How do the children get to be so confident about their own organization and choices?'

Staff would explain their ways of planning and organizing the group to meet these responsibilities. In each case it seems that there are separate stages of staff activity involved – planning and providing resources in advance, noting and thinking about children's use of the provision, and making new plans as a result of the children's behaviour. Explanations come as answers to the questions that spring to the visitor's mind.

How do you know what children will want?

A wide range of activities is put out each day and a record is kept of what has been used and how popular it was. Certain children have particular interests that staff bear in mind, and staff also relate what is on offer today to the things children were doing before or to noteworthy happenings like a recent visit from a new baby. This provokes the question 'How do the staff know so much about the children?' The answer to this is

1. Parents – the apparently purely social chats on entering and leaving are important exchanges of information as well;
2. Watching children, thinking about them, talking about them with other members of staff;
3. Keeping detailed brief records of what has happened in each child's day, and keeping this record up to date regularly;
4. Building up a collection of evidence of each child's work, including drawings and paintings that the child is willing to spare, copies of others, photos of models and brick-work, photos of outdoor activities and notes of conversations with the child. These collections are regularly discussed with child and parent and comments by both recorded.

This explanation about the need for careful attention to recording children's progress goes some way to answer the next question.

How can you be certain that children are learning when you don't directly teach them?

The visitor first has to be reassured that direct teaching does indeed have a place in nursery work. A music session was in progress when the visitor arrived, but may not have been noticed because it was in the form of a game. A small group of three or four children were gathered around a nursery nurse, who was introducing them to some instruments. She held up the instrument, asked its name, and showed how it was played. Each child then had a chance to handle it, repeat its name and say how it was played – blown, banged, shaken, plucked and so on. Next a song was sung while an instrument was passed around – 'Take the tambourine, pass it on, pass it on, pass it on, Take the tambourine, pass it on, whose turn's next?' Later each child has an instrument and they all play together, experimenting with loud and soft sounds.

The teaching is carefully planned for the children's needs. These are new entrants to the class, some of whom are barely two, and they have to be introduced to many new ideas, such as waiting for their turn, while being made to feel that they matter as individuals. The game helps to teach that in an enjoyable way, and a further stage of the music provision, later in the week, might include a session on rhythm where the children clap to the rhythm of their own and each other's names.

How do you monitor children's progress ?

Whether they are engaged in direct teaching or not, practitioners monitor children's progress through noting what they do. Throughout the mixture of spontaneous and directed activities staff keep careful records of what each child achieves in various ways so that they can tell what they are learning and monitor their progress. In the music session, two children are at the stage of playing their instruments without being much aware of the idea of stopping and starting together. They have to be reminded to stop individually. Others have got the idea through imitating the nursery nurse, and copy her every gesture as she holds her instrument high to show that she has stopped. There is a further stage too – all of these children are at a different point from a child who watches the nursery nurse's actions and, when she stops and raises her arms in the air, lays down his instrument and says 'I stopping, look, I stopping!'

Spontaneous activities are also rich in opportunities to gather information about children. In a nursery following the Desirable Outcomes, four-year-old Giles, for instance, has been noted as being interested in numbers – he is always keen to help with jobs that involve counting, such as laying the table, but he does it by taking a handful of knives and putting one by each place-mat until finished. He cannot yet count the mats and then fetch the right number of knives. Staff feel this is quite normal – he is making good progress. He is building up his understanding of numbers. Records are kept about other aspects of children's development as well. The learning environment is planned so that all sorts of different things can be learned from each activity. Giles is playing in wet sand at present; he is 'driving my truck' up and down, admiring the tracks it leaves. The experience is rich in language for him as he talks to another child about trucks he has seen on the roads and what they do. The shape and depth of the tracks stimulates him to think about how wet sand holds its shape and how other materials like water and dry sand do not – they are available to try – and he talks about the direction and changes of shape he can cause by different movements.

How do the children become so confident about their own organization and choices?

The visitor finds the children very friendly but is a bit overwhelmed by the self-sufficiency with which they organize their time and their social relationships. Staff say that this does not happen at once in every case – children often take a while to feel confident about making their own choices. Once they have made a friend they usually take off on their own together. The new ones and those children who are having any kind of worry may need a bit of adult encouragement to make independent choices, and they all need adults to play and work alongside them. Staff try to be aware of what children are doing so they can further their ideas – Giles has been introduced to the idea of painting the wheels and running the truck over paper to mark the tracks, their direction and the shape they leave behind. Riding a tricycle through a puddle in the playground might come next if he is still interested, or big blocks of playground chalk to mark where children can walk.

In the classroom a story such as the old favourite *Rosie's Walk* (Hutchins, 1968) will enable him to relate his own experience to published material, which he can retell and comment on to other children and adults. This way of building on children's own ideas and interests gives them the confidence that they have something worthwhile to offer, and it does not limit the curriculum – far from it. Giles, and the other children who take an interest in what is going on, are learning about spatial relationships and getting ideas about patterns and about early mapmaking. The language that they are learning to use will enable them to put into words their ideas about space, direction, shape, perspective and so on. In the course of their enjoyable play, they are beginning to see the usefulness of signs and symbols. Giles turns a corner with his truck and lifts it from the paper or the sand; underneath lies a mark that he can, with adult help, copy to make a sign in the playground to show where wheeled traffic must turn carefully at the sharp corner by the hut. Later, some words could be added. This sign could be an entry into the world of representing real things on paper, and an entry into the real world of road signs and their accompanying messages. It can also be part of provision for learning through self-motivated play which takes in many of the requirements of the Desirable Outcomes and the National Curriculum (see pp. 11–12, for an example).

The curriculum for this group is well-founded in terms of the subject disciplines, in that staff are aware of the scientific, geographical, mathematical, linguistic and literacy content of Giles' experiences. They are also able to draw on child development insights, in that they can see the connections in his mind between an imaginative game of being a truck-driver and learning about direction, angle and length. It is the uniting of these two strands that give this kind of education the conceptual strength and the flexibility to meet the needs of many different children. It is this view of the curriculum as evolving through the interaction of adult and child which is the key ingredient in successful educational provision for this age-group.

And what about the other children? After discussing Giles in such detail it may seem as if staff are providing a curriculum for one child, while others can join in if they wish, or as if staff will wear themselves out providing twenty separate curricula. In the group, however, children both learn from and with each other, so that an input of the kind that interests and stretches Giles will be of great interest to others who can incorporate it into what they are doing. Staff who see their interest can then think how to make an input that would benefit them. Donna and Marie watched Giles in the playground and in the classroom they made a picture of how to get to the seaside. Staff provided little suitcases and they packed up the home corner dolls and set off. Two other girls were being bus drivers and they had a bus in the classroom, with seats for passengers and a steering wheel. Staff talked with them about where they were going, where to turn, how to get to Sainsbury's and so on.

The newcomer at this point may well feel a bit confused. Can it be education if you let children choose what they learn? Is it enough to let the adults become record-keepers for the children's progress – should they not be deciding what the children ought to learn?

These are sensible points, and ones which are important in the education of even the youngest children. Staff explain that although children have a free choice of what is there, what is provided is carefully chosen to give educational opportunities, including the society of other children and adults. In the baby room, there are different resources available all the time, and the adults watch to see which babies show an interest in. Turning the head to watch other children go by shows that the baby is tired of the cot toys and wants some human company; babies of a very young age enjoy interacting with other babies and develop responsive friendships (Goldschmied and Selleck, 1996). As soon as they can sit up, babies can be given a range of objects to choose from, and encouraged to explore them with other children.

Children do not have the freedom to choose things that are not there, nor are they allowed to do things that are dangerous or upsetting to others. They are also positively encouraged in certain directions by staff as they play and work alongside them, and by extension provided through staff planning new ideas. In a room where some children are just beginning to walk, toddlers have a selection of apparatus for climbing up, over and through, but it is not put out all at once. The nursery workers watch to see what activities children prefer to engage in, and they make sure that the apparatus is there on a regular basis, extending the activity by adding to it. Recently, children have been practising going up and down steps; the staff have found a set of low steps leading to a small platform which children can climb up to and get down from. When they feel an extension is needed, they could add a low slide to the far side, or they could exchange the apparatus for some sturdy wooden boxes to climb on; some of these are hollow, so that children can go through or over them. The children are practising their climbing skills and balance; they are enjoying playing with the hollow boxes, hiding from each other or getting in together; they are also having practical experience of going up, over and down, going in, through and out, being above or below someone, being together and being on their own.

Careful observation of the children will show how they are each using these opportunities and what would be good ways to provide their next learning experiences. A nursery centre has created a small hill in its playground. Children who have enjoyed climbing up the steps in their room have the chance now to take their learning about different levels onwards. A child with a learning disability crawled to the top over and over again, giving his key-worker the clue that now was a good time to help him transfer learning about going down from the wooden steps to a grassy slope. Even with very young children, practitioners need to think about how the learning environment, in and out of doors, can give children a broad, exciting and challenging range of opportunities to learn more about the world, themselves and other people.

Creating an environment that challenges children to learn

When they plan an indoor and outdoor learning environment that will be broad, balanced and stimulating for children, practitioners have to plan on the basis of a sort of learning model of the world. The sorts of things they want children to learn determine what they provide for children to play with, and they determine also how they help them to learn as they play and explore. Children become more proficient explorers and more imaginative in their play as they get to grips with the planned learning environment. In this way, they are making choices, but the adults make sure that they are educational ones that have been planned for.

An environment planned in this way should, for instance, reflect the practitioners' awareness of the importance of the active processes of investigating, examining and creating. It should also reflect understanding of the importance of the different disciplines of knowledge – language and literacy and all the others. Resources for digging or looking through magnifiers are available, various natural materials like stones are supplied for handling, and there are books for reference. Children seem to be expected to use books and to write and draw freely. They are encouraged to tell stories and to listen to them. Play is provided for in several different areas, including outdoors, through dressing up, home corner, small world equipment, etc. Children can make things with wood at a carpentry bench, use different kinds of paint and make models. Clay is set out with tools beside it on the table. Construction materials, big and little, are put out to use, as are puzzles. There are musical instruments, and games to do with number. The visitor can see that there are certain different kinds of knowledge embodied in the environment – scientific, mathematical, linguistic and literary, creative, technological and artistic. In addition to these different disciplines, the learning environment implies that learning is active – you do not sit there waiting for it to happen – and that you make your own choices about what you do.

Observation, assessment, evaluation and planning

This approach to learning demands a thoughtful approach to the educational experiences offered to young children. At its heart lie constant assessment and evaluation based on observation which is the early childhood practitioner's most formidable skill. From what has been described above it will be seen that only scrupulous observation and record-keeping, with plans and provision of resources based on this, could allow the staff to offer appropriate experiences to a large group of young children.

This is a very important educational idea. This kind of education shows itself as a model of the way in which the teaching and learning processes interact. It makes clear the good-practice base on which all quality of education depends throughout the early years. Quality of content in terms of the knowledge, understanding and skills that staff offer to children has to be matched by quality of understanding of the learner, through which decisions about the curriculum are made.

The newcomer may have been wondering how practitioners come to make decisions about what to do, or do they simply wait until children show an interest? This would result in a very bitty kind of planning, surely? This is the complicated bit – staff explain that they know the sort of thing to do to give children opportunities they can use. They know that there are kinds of knowledge, understanding and skills that children need to have. They know that the opportunities provided should embody the knowledge, understanding and skills needed in a way that children can relate to. Lastly, they know that they can adapt and develop what they provide through their planning so that the individual children will be interested in it. An example from the previous term is given.

Planning from children's use of blocks

Children are routinely provided with large wooden blocks of different sizes, and planks to go with them. They are known to use these in a variety of ways, sometimes for the sheer pleasure of building structures which fit together and stand up, sometimes to be a castle, house or boat. Often the building is a part of some kind of play. Staff took trouble to redesign the block area, to make sure it was spacious, untroubled by people passing through, and equipped with suitable play items for the likely kinds of use. Three girls took all the blocks and planks and spent more than an hour trying to make a seat which was evenly balanced and which would support their weight. They needed help part way through, because they had difficulty getting a symmetrical support for each side, although they understood about supporting both ends of the seat. At last they were successful, and they summoned their teacher to come and try it out. Staff had provided the blocks and planks in an attractive way because they knew of the opportunities for play, language, technological thinking and so on that they could offer. The way the girls had used them provided a base from which to make further block provision in the coming weeks. The unobtrusive addition of some furniture from the home corner encouraged the girls to think about more building work, and they made a boat with a flat, raft-like base and separate compartments for people to sit in. Smaller seats incorporated some principles from the seat-building, and the experience in fitting different sizes of blocks together was also useful. Gura (1992) has shown from work in nursery and infant classrooms how complex and intellectually challenging children's work with blocks can be when practitioners give it priority, which means seeing it as a real part of the curriculum and observing to see what children are learning from it. It also means giving the blockplay room (it needs a lot, and an undisturbed site), resources (good blocks are expensive), time (uninterrupted and continued from day to day so that ideas can develop) and adult support to ensure that all children see it as valuable and that all children have a chance to use it.

Developing provision for learning

The developing of provision over a long period of time is the way in which staff try to avoid a 'bitty' alternation of ideas. A nursery school staff could give an example of their provision for growing plants. In the spring they planned to make a garden in the outdoor play area, and asked for parent help with digging and fertilizing straight away so that it would be ready for planting at the end of April. With the children they consulted parents, some of whom had very green fingers or gardening connections, about what would grow. They borrowed books and magazine articles to see what was recommended, and worked with the children to decide what it would be best to choose. Everyone examined the plot to see if it was a suitable size for what they had chosen, and marked out how many rows of vegetables and so on they could have. This very practical approach, which involved the children, staff and parents in planning, consulting the drawings, photographs and plans in reference books, mapping out the plots by drawing measured lines with a stick and counting them, had in it lots of educational value. The children discussed the number of rows, the different kinds of crops – someone's grandad grows potatoes and someone else's grandad has hens that lay green eggs when the grass is new. They talked about the fact that it was too early to plant outdoors yet although the grandad who grew potatoes showed them how to start the seed potatoes 'chitting' so they would be ready when it was time for planting. Children looked at the packets of seed with the bright pictures on them, noting the different colours, shapes and sizes. Reading the packets with parents gave experience of specialist language in addition to 'chitting'. Some packets suggested starting seeds indoors, and there was discussion of whether the classroom was the right kind of environment, and what children and staff would have to remember to do to keep them going through the half-term break.

Some of the vegetables on the packets were familiar – carrots, potatoes and onions, for instance, featured in many children's dinners at home. Speculation mounted when an adult introduced the idea of eating what they grew at school for school dinner, and Edward (see p. 14–16) said they had carrots at home but he never ate anything like that.

Just this one planning aspect of the planting project seemed to staff to include the elements required by the Desirable Outcomes, as well as the HMI Areas of Experience (DES, 1989c) from which they had been planning before and which they wanted to go on using to ensure a broad curriculum.

Beyond the purely subject orientation, this way of providing education offers the chance for children to feel, smell, dig, handle, make visual estimations and so on. They can bring their previous experience, and their home lives in particular, to bear on it. They will see something real come of something talked about and planned in advance. They will have a shared experience which will go on for more than a term in various ways, even if the crops are not much to eat in the end. The sharpness of spring onions or radishes, the excitement of digging potatoes in order to wash and cook them for lunch, will outweigh any other shortcomings. They will be able to make something real and useful happen by their own efforts, which will contribute to meeting a real need for food. They will see how living plants grow and are cared for in a natural environment.

This was a good beginning, but the development also had to be planned. The staff certainly had their own ideas, based on their previous experience of young children and on their understanding of the subject disciplines. The development would be partly on that basis, and partly from what was learned from looking at the children's responses. How the children's responses develop makes clear what can be done next. The newcomer might be worried that they would all do different things, but in fact they do not each do something different. Some children will like to play at having a garden centre, which means one kind of provision. Others will want to be gardeners, which will affect the use of the outdoor environment. Many will focus on the little creatures discovered in digging, and a 'minibeasts' theme will be set up. Some will not want to do any of these things, but will share a story on the theme of growing things and eating them. Others might construct imaginative play on the theme of what is underneath the ground – anything from dinosaur bones to buried treasure could be their theme. Meeting these responses with further extensions would not be too overwhelming, and would fit in well with the normal sort of provision like clay, puzzles, imaginative play provision and blocks.

There is a place for staff initiatives in daily planning and in further extensions of plans, and there must be, if the learning that takes place in the group is to be built upon. Understanding of the learning process and of the particular learners in question is, as we saw earlier, only half of the professional expertise. The other half is concerned with our knowledge and understanding about the world and the disciplines of knowledge through which we organize our learning. Staff make decisions about the learning environment by relating these two aspects of their expertise. This is done through planning which relates new approaches or ideas to the existing context, to children's ideas and interests and to their responses to previous provision. Observation, assessment and record-keeping must therefore play an extremely important part, providing the source of ideas about further development of the curriculum as well as about children's progress.

Planning and responding in this way means that from their previous observation and assessment adults know what it is that children are ready for. From day to day this can be modified so that continuity is ensured with children's interests. As an example, one member of staff recounts the not uncommon experience of giving a child a worm to hold while digging. When she turned her back to go on digging she heard his voice say 'Look, now I've got two worms!' The gardening activity was swiftly extended to how to look after small creatures as well as plants. This was not just a strategy for teaching ways to handle living creatures, but a genuine development in which understanding about how to handle plants could be generalized to other living things. In both the advance and the day-to-day planning, record-keeping is extremely important because it embodies the planning, monitoring and assessment processes.

An 'early years' curriculum and the National Curriculum

This responsive curriculum, which is based on the observation and assessment of individual children, can inform our thinking about the National Curriculum. Children below statutory age are not required to take part in the National Curriculum but in the light of the difference between it and the early years curriculum it is as well to reflect on how the two can be related to each other. We can think back to Giles, learning about numbers at his own pace through practical experience, and see the importance of this process in his learning. Knowledge of child development helps staff to understand that he needs to build up his learning at his own pace. The younger children are the more vital it is that they are offered a curriculum which responds to their developmental needs.

There may be pressure from various sources to alter what is done at the age of four in order to 'get children ready'. We must be aware that the National Curriculum can impinge heavily on younger children. There may be pressure to 'prepare' children for it, but we cannot prepare children for an athletic future by making them do the programmes for older children. Rather, we need to prepare them by making sure they have rewarding experiences of success at their own levels now, to give them strength and confidence for the future. This is what a good education in the years before five should do, and the education of older children should build on these achievements.

In giving children the best quality of education that we can, we must not forget that we need to help them also to get the best of it for themselves. The second way in which a good early years curriculum is important is that it prepares children for a challenging and high-quality educational experience, in which they are expected to be active in their own learning and to make sensible choices. Because of the way that children are given choices, for instance, they learn to be responsible. Children will get from this the notion that they are expected to be active and involved in their own education – a useful approach throughout life. This is not a simple task and requires sensitive handling by staff. Children can often need help to learn how to use the educational advantages of this new social situation, which is full of opportunities but also can be bewildering.

Unless this transition from home to learning in a group setting is successfully achieved there may be considerable problems in the child's later attitude to education. Aspects of the child's emotional and social development are involved in the process of getting to know how to use educational opportunities. The difficulties that may be experienced by children when this happens could lead to a child being alienated from the educational process in various ways. The invisible quiet child is just as worrying as the one who is disruptive.

Two different children were trying to come to terms with being part of a group of children in a class. Both had encountered some difficulties, but one protested frantically and one was quietly despairing.

Maria's mother and father both worked, and her grandmother had looked after her during the day until now. She had just begun to settle her in the class. The home language was Portuguese; the grandmother spoke little English, but the parents were both fluent in English. Maria, who spoke very little English, was understandably anxious about being on her own in the class. After four weeks staff became concerned when she still would not let her grandmother out of her sight and could not bear her to leave the room for a minute. Staff acquired some strategic words of Portuguese, but Maria remained very unsettled. If the grandmother went out, even to go to the toilet, Maria became distraught; she screamed and fought, and then vomited.

Edward had been coming to the group for six months. He felt very unhappy about his father leaving him, but he did not protest violently. He expressed himself by standing silently in tears exactly where he had been left. His only other plea for attention was in refusing to eat any food at lunchtime. Mornings and home-times were fraught for all connected with these children. Edward was 4 years 6 months, Maria was just a year younger. It was clear to staff and parents that both children had understandable reasons for finding it hard to part. Maria was naturally anxious about being on her own in an English-speaking group, and this was compounded by differences of opinion at home about how to deal with her anxiety – whether to be sympathetic or to discourage her from this behaviour. Edward's family had suffered stress because of his father's unemployment, and he displayed a lot of anxiety if it was ever suggested that he be away from his parents, even for an enjoyable treat with a neighbour. Meals were a battleground at home, and his parents were very worried about this. Parents and staff were able to decide on a united approach. Each child needed different treatment, and staff worked over a period of two terms to help them and their families with their difficulties.

The slow building up of personal relationships with staff in which the children's needs were recognized was thought to be the key to both children's feelings of security. Maria did not need someone to speak Portuguese to her as long as she felt that her particular needs were going to be met. Her grandmother explained that she often vomited when she was upset, and that at home they gave her a drink of water to calm her down. Staff adopted this as a procedure, and gradually Maria began to find it easier to part from her grandmother. She began to accept that she would always get the drink to calm her down after her grandmother left and that staff could be relied on to help her in other ways she found acceptable. Almost one year later she saw the staff member who had been involved most with her but who had later left the group. She recognized her, came across the playground smiling and said 'I drink water', before she went off on her own business again. Edward did not show a sudden transformation but he gradually began to become more at ease when he was asked to choose precisely what he would like to eat. The two peas and a dab of tomato sauce that he wanted at first were given to him. This was reassuring, and it also appealed to his sense of humour. He enjoyed the way the other children found it amusing but accepted it as right for him. These miniscule helpings never blossomed into a full plate but he seemed to feel safer now that he could control exactly what he ate. He began to talk to staff and to make some progress with other children.

Many children have problems getting used to education in a group. These two were extreme cases, but not that unusual. If their worries were not faced and dealt with at an early stage, when they were most responsive and there was a good staff ratio, the whole of their infant education might have been spent trying to overcome their fears. A single-handed infant teacher in a classroom would have had great pressure imposed on him or her by their needs, the children's learning would have been seriously interrupted, and the first and formative stages of their education would have been associated in their minds with distress. Each could have suffered in a different way. Quiet, withdrawn children learn how to avoid getting involved in classroom activities by not attracting attention and later can become early drop-outs. On the other hand angry, desperate children attract all too much attention – they put great energy into defeating the aims of teachers and parents for their education and make life harder for all around them in school.

Conclusion

It is better educationally, and easier organizationally, to teach children through what they are concerned about. The early years curriculum is founded on developmental principles which guide us in making choices about how to teach children. In this chapter we have been focusing on how young children's access to the curriculum depends on the capacity of practitioners to make appropriate decisions about presenting opportunities for learning. In the next chapter, we will try to think through what this means in terms of children's deepest concerns – their relationships and experiences with parents and family, their exploratory activity from birth, their drive to play, to understand, to make connections and to communicate with others.

Further reading

Blenkin, G. M. and Whitehead, M. R. (1996) Creating a context for development in G. M. Blenkin and A. V. Kelly (eds.) *Early Childhood Education: a Developmental Curriculum*, Paul Chapman, London.
Bruce, T. (1987) *Early Childhood Education*, Hodder and Stoughton, London.
Early Years Curriculum Group (1992) *First Things First; Educating Young Children*, Madeleine Lindley, Oldham.

For discussion

Each of the references listed above includes a set of developmental principles to which the author or authors subscribe. Take one such set and analyse it. Does it reflect all that you would consider important in early education? How does it compare with your own principles?

2

Young Children Thinking

The rapid pace of economic, social and industrial change today demands that education should prepare children for the intelligent use of their understanding rather than the unthinking application of unchanging ideas about the world. Fostering children's potential for creativity, adaptability and independent thinking is not only in the children's interests; we need them to have these abilities for our own benefit as well. Our future will depend on their capacity to think independently and creatively, and as practitioners we should seek to increase these qualities and to promote mental adaptability in children of every age and stage. If this is to be done, all practitioners must scrutinize and question their practice to ensure that they are not underestimating children and limiting rather than enhancing their achievements. In order to do this, we need to know children well as individuals, and understand something of the home experiences, relationships and language in which their thinking is rooted.

This lays a heavy responsibility on those who educate children of whatever age. It is vital to educational success to think about how the provision for children at every stage of their education can reflect this approach. In the early years long-lasting attitudes to intellectual activity are being laid down. What is learned about the extent to which people value independence of thought at this stage will often last throughout a child's school career. For the early years practitioner this means learning about how very young children's thinking develops and about how different kinds of educational provision will have different effects on their ability to use their minds.

How children think and learn

It has long been believed that there are significant differences between the way young children think and learn and the way that adults experience learning. This belief can tend towards under-estimation of children's capacities, and can apparently justify giving children boring and repetitious things to do – things which adults would find intolerable themselves. Again, the work of Piaget has been taken to show that the gradual building up of understanding of the world means that young children have problems with logical processes – that the main point of his investigations is that they cannot 'do' certain mental operations. This condemns children to a 'basic skills' approach, where they have to grind their way through specific operations without knowing how they are of use, and learn dislocated segments of knowledge without being able to apply them to satisfy their immediate needs. This interpretation ignores the evidence that Piaget's studies contribute towards our picture of the child as ceaselessly active in constructing mental models of how things work from experience of the world, and testing these ideas against present reality.

> The principle to which we are referring consists then in regarding the child not as a being of pure imitation, but as an organism which assimilates things to itself, selects them and digests them according to its own structure. In this way even what is influenced by the adult may still be original.
>
> (Piaget, 1973, p. 40)

Moreover, much recent work has pointed to the similarities between children's and adults' thinking rather than the differences (see, for instance, Donaldson, 1978) and there now seems to be room for the idea that what is different is the limited nature of children's experience rather than the quality of their mental processes. Some of their understandings of natural phenomena, for instance, are informed by their own personal experience alone, and therefore do not benefit from a full range of past experience or from the informed views of experts. Alan, interrupted while racing out into the playground without a coat in January, expostulated 'But the sun's shining – it's hot out there!'

There is another way in which children's thinking may present itself as being qualitatively different from that of adults, while not being so fundamentally different as it appears. This is in relation to their use of physical movements and visual markings to express their understanding of aspects of the world around them. Matthews (1994) has shown that children's drawing and painting begins with movements which express and indeed actually organize their thinking. His observations of his own children's self-expression from birth form the basis of a picture of children using their developing capacity for both large and small movements to express, in body movements and graphically, their ideas and experiences.

From a detailed examination of children's responses to their experience we can see them applying reasoning developed from previous experience. They are developing rules by which to interpret what happens or to forecast what is likely to happen. Donaldson and McGarrigle (Donaldson, 1978) showed that once a problem made sense to children they were able to deal with it intellectually. Other researchers such as Wells (1985, 1987) and

In a nursery school, Maireaid, 4 years 3 months, used a painting of a rough oval to represent a circling aircraft, then adapted the oval shape for use in paintings which represented her family, naming dots of paint that she placed inside the shape as mother, father, brothers and baby. Simultaneously, Nedjemedine, 4 years 6 months, encircled items of equipment on a bicycle in the playground and went in and out of a small gate between sections of the playground, calling to adults that he was outside or coming back in. (For more details see Early Years Curriculum Group, 1989.) These patterns and others of the same kind direct attention to children's efforts to organize their experience of the world; they are far from the ways in which adults are used to thinking about their own experiences, and yet in their search for one unifying characteristic by which to describe a phenomenon they show more kinship than dissimilarity with adult conceptual activity. Maireaid's painting expressed in visual terms what the phrase 'nuclear family' means; Nedjemedine was playing with being inside and outside his own class space in rather similar terms. The idea of 'sorting', which means placing like with like, is both a mathematical and a logical activity. At infant school children are often asked to group together similar objects, sometimes inside a circle the teacher has drawn. Here, the children were doing this by themselves, and in a way that few adults might have deliberately thought up. The spontaneous nature of this activity, in which readers may well see much else of interest, shows that adults can learn from children how much they have achieved already in their thinking about the world.

Wood (1988) have also seen the difficulties as being located in the language or the materials in which adults have sought to test children's capacity to think. This suggests that we must find ways to teach that make sense to the young child. It is for the adults to use their powers of observation and their insight to discover what ideas children are exploring.

The important role of the adult

This is not as easy as it sounds, for adults tend to cling to their own notions of what education is and often find it hard to be sufficiently adaptable to the child's patterns of thought. Educating the young child is very frequently thought of in terms of teaching concepts such as the basics of colour, letters, numbers and shapes – this has probably given rise to the belief that there is no great intellectual challenge for adults engaged in education in the years before compulsory school. In fact the concepts that young children develop may make use of visible qualities of objects such as number, colour, shape and size but they tend to employ them as building blocks in far more sophisticated patterns which make great demands on adult understanding. Young children's thinking about the world uses every tool available to handle the fundamental issues of their lives, but adults have to listen carefully and think creatively to catch the messages. If adults can perceive what children are saying through their representations of their thinking, they can see that these representations show how they are inveterate users of logical systems, and how their attention is drawn to anything which appears contrary to the logic they are using. A girl of four made a joke on this basis. She drew one large shape and several small ones around it, like a mother hen with chicks or a mother with children. When asked if she would like something written down on her picture she said 'The little ones are fooding the big one!'

A child of 20 months at home puts on her father's shoes and trudges carefully down the stairs. Her mother says 'You're wearing Daddy's shoes! They're too big for you, aren't they?' The child says 'Big shoes! Daddy gone to the shops . . . Daddy come back soon?' For the mother, with her parental closeness to the child, the response 'Yes, he's not going to be long, he's only gone to the DIY shop to get some paint' comes easily. This meets the child's meaning because it responds to the message about what the father is

doing and relates to ideas about adults, their size and powerful-
ness, their roles, and their comings and goings in the lives of their
children. The discussion that follows this exchange focuses on
what is going to be painted and why.

We can see the difference between a formal educational response and a creative one, such as that of the mother here. She
knows that the child is thinking about her father as a whole – the
size of his shoes, his absence at the shops, his reasons for going to
the shops, his contribution to maintaining the home. The mother's
replies to the child are not random, but focused on the real area of
interest. Compare this with the common situation where a child
has a new item of clothing to show off. 'Look at my socks!' he says,
and awaits the response. The stock answer would be to ask what
colour they are, and what else he can see that is that colour. A reply
that was focused on what mattered to the child would try to find
out what was most important about the socks to him – perhaps
'Those are nice, aren't they. How did you get them?' This leaves
room to find out what the child feels are the salient features of the
socks.

In a small way, this example illustrates the dilemma of the educators of very young children. The educators need to construct a
curriculum built on the real life of the children, because that is how
they learn. Parents are mightily influential educators because they
are such vital features of children's lives. Wells has described some
of the qualities of what he calls 'home-talk'. He writes of

> a number of important qualities that characterise the sort of con-
> versational experience which leads to effective use of language by
> children:
>
> 1. A warm responsiveness to the child's interests and a recognition
>   of the child as an autonomous individual with valid purposes
>   and ways of seeing things,
> 2. Negotiation of meaning and purpose in the joint construction of
>   an inter-subjective reality,
> 3. An invitation to the child to consider the immediate present in
>   a wider framework of intention and consequence, feelings and
>   principles.
>
> (Wells, 1983, p. 132)

The rest of us have to go to great lengths to link up with children's
thoughts and feelings in the same sort of way, which is why there
is such a strong emphasis on observation and record-keeping in
the early years curriculum. As practitioners, we are fortunate that

young children are curious about us, and usually willing to give us at least a chance to show whether we are warm, responsive and interesting people to be with. This is why so much of the work of the nursery practitioner is concerned with children's all-round well-being (see, for instance, Edgington, forthcoming 1998, on the nursery teacher as carer and educator of young children). We are also fortunate in that parents are usually very willing to help us get to know their children, if we will take advantage of our opportunities to make friends with them and learn from them (see Chapter 3 for more about parents).

The crucial difference between good and inadequate provision for early learning is the difference between real meaning and artificiality. We need to learn how this distinction should affect our approach to teaching children, and what qualities we need to develop as practitioners in order to foster high-level intellectual activity.

Interactive education

Wells (1987, for instance) has pointed out repeatedly how easy it is for adults to fail to respond to children at their own more complex level if they retain a view of education as being one-sided. He states that we must see education as a joint venture.

> A fuller understanding of the nature of linguistic interaction, whether at home or in the classroom, is leading us to recognise that to be most effective the relationship between teacher and learner must, at every stage of development, be collaborative. Teaching, thus seen, is not a didactic transmission of pre-formulated knowledge, but an attempt to negotiate shared meanings and understandings.
>
> (Wells, 1985, p. 73)

Negotiated learning

For the educator of young children, the problems inherent in this statement are great. There is no parental closeness to assist the adult in understanding the child's message, and there are many children in the group. Would it not be simpler to accept defeat? This is what is implied in the view of early education as being about learning a certain number of limited formal skills and memorizing letter and number shapes. This is also inherent in the judgement that group sizes do not affect children's learning. Yet if we want early education to support children in being vigorous, inventive, practical and enterprising thinkers and doers we must not give in to defeatism. Somehow we must find ways to teach in co-ordination with the characteristic ways in which learning in humans takes place.

Vygotsky (1978) has shown how deeply social our learning is, and has constructed a picture of the adult as the one who assists the child to achieve today what it will be possible to achieve unaided tomorrow. Goldschmied and Selleck (1996) and Goldschmied (1992 and 1993) have recorded on video the social interactions of babies and children under two as they learn together and alongside each other. Unless we wish to abdicate our responsibility for providing appropriate learning opportunities, we have to try to meet the challenge posed by grouping children in educational settings outside the home.

Unlikely as it may seem, it is possible to approach working with young children in groups as a collaborative venture, and it is much the most stimulating approach for both adults and children. It leads to insights into what we mean by the word 'teaching' and into what we mean when we plan for the education of our children, as will be seen in the discussion of the curriculum in Chapter 4. The essence of this approach is to give the children the tools they need for learning so that the practitioners are free to observe, assess and evaluate their learning, and respond to them in ways that will lead that learning further. The planned indoor and outdoor learning environment is the starting-point for the whole process.

Constructing the learning environment

In order to work with children in this collaborative way, adults have to build a learning environment which children can use to suit their own purposes, without being told what to do and without having to ask if they want to use equipment or materials, to go outside or indoors, to have a drink or go to the toilet. The environment must offer children what they need for learning; as human learning is essentially a social process, the learning environment must foster and support relationships between children and between children and adults, as well as stimulating children's powers of communication, expression, thinking, creativity and curiosity about the world around them. The essential ingredient is in the 'empowering' of the pupil. Without the children taking on some of the responsibility for what goes on there will be no possibility of the adult having the freedom to work with individuals or small groups, and without the adult's preparedness to learn from the children's self-originated activity there will be no focus on their learning processes. The careful advance organization of the learning environment to make it possible for children to develop their own interests takes a great burden from the adult. The way in which 'subject' knowledge and skills help practitioners in structuring a coherent learning environment is discussed in Chapter 5. More will be said about the detailed resourcing of the environment later (see pp. 68–70). Here it is the intentions behind the creation of the 'self-winding' learning environment which are explored.

In this approach it is the children who should decide what they are going to do and with whom, and the adults who try to help social relationships develop, and ensure that the selection of opportunities that is available provides a balanced and stimulating

> In a session where a group were exploring materials prepared according to this approach, a child of 18 months picked up a length of chain from the pile of chains. He picked up a cardboard tube and, holding it in his left hand, tried to dangle the end of the chain over it and down into it. This operation was too difficult for him, so he put down the tube and picked up a metal canister. The wider mouth made it possible for him to achieve his goal, and he spent the next five minutes putting the chain in, watching how it coiled itself as he lowered it, and then taking it out again, watching to see how it uncoiled in exact reverse order. Identifying the characteristics of the chain challenges this child to find words to express what it is he likes about the chain and its behaviour. Finding a container large enough and noting the coiling and uncoiling sequence highlights mathematical facts about size, about things fitting or not fitting inside and about exact reversability. The characteristics and behaviour of the chain in comparison with that of the cardboard tube and the metal canister draw attention to how materials can be similar to and different from each other, and to the practical implications of these similarities and differences for what the child wanted to do. Without being able to hear from the child how he would describe what he was engaged in doing, it is clear that valuable experiences were being encountered.

range of learning opportunities. Many valuable things are learned in this way – children learn that adults respect their decisions, that they want them to be able to make their own input in classroom and playground, that they are under no compulsion to produce anything to show, but that the adults do value the end-products if there are any as well as the learning and enjoyment during the activity.

Goldschmied has developed an approach for babies (1993) and for children under two (1992) which is based on making time, space, materials and adult support when needed available for children so that they can explore appropriate materials. Goldschmied and Jackson (1994) see these early exploratory activities as giving children the information that they need about the world and the physical and mental skills needed for processing and building on this information. Language, mathematics, technology and science are rooted in this kind of experience.

As children get older, it is easier for adults to understand the uses, imaginative and practical, to which they are putting materials, and we can also see how they continue to learn from them. Through following their own interests in a planned learning environment children learn about the resources and equipment too; they learn about their uses on their own and in combination. They learn how they are stored, and this, like all grouping and ordering processes, teaches about the underlying structure of thinking that governs their storage. When children and adults are exploring the place where science equipment and resources are stored, looking at, handling and reflecting on the different items, we are encountering some of the most important things that can be learned about scientific ways of investigating, thinking about and knowing the world around us. The tools for observing, researching, identifying, weighing, measuring, recording and so on tell us that science is an empirical discipline, whose truths are defined as being externally verifiable. They tell us that the world is investigated using the senses; that it is to be observed, described and recorded; that it can be very precisely weighed and measured, but that it can also be represented in drawings, diagrams and words; that much of it requires particular care in investigation because all living things are to be respected and valued; that much of great interest is hidden from us without special equipment for perceiving it. The books and displays that should be near show how we can place our own experiences and discoveries in the context of others' knowledge that has been built up in the course of many lifetimes. More practically, children learn how resources and equipment have to be maintained, about how materials must be returned to the expected place if they are to be available again and about how one can choose particular resources according to their suitability for the purpose in hand.

While children explore the environment and use it for their own purposes, the practitioner's intentions and knowledge are informing this active learning with a much wider perspective which leads towards the school disciplines of knowledge. While this encounter with the foundations of the disciplines is going on, practitioners can give attention to individual children and to what they are thinking and learning in a way that they could not if they were busy giving direct instruction, or trying to get children to behave in different ways from their natural learning processes.

Attending to individuals

Thus, an environment planned for children's independent use will free adults for the important part of their work, which is the collaborative work with individuals and small groups. The following instance may give some idea of the kind of activity adults need to be free to engage in if all children are to have a good chance of educational progress and development. This is particularly important in the case of children who have special needs of any kind; at this very early stage of development short-term learning difficulties can often be effectively remedied before they cause permanent harm, or, if they are long-term in their impact, strategies for helping children with them can be developed.

Ricardo, 4 years 5 months, was a child who gave staff and his mother many worried moments. He seemed to be angry almost all the time, both at home and at school. His anger seemed to well up at school with little if any provocation, and his moods could switch unexpectedly. For instance, he might be sitting at the table at dinner time as food was brought over, apparently calm, and then suddenly he might push his chair furiously back from the table and shout 'No!' Children would look up, startled, and he would roar at them, 'Don't look at me'. His relationships with other children were not good, except for one friend, with whom he would make plans which sometimes remained secret and sometimes led to confrontations with children or practitioners. Staff were frustrated and puzzled, but they also noticed that within this child there were great talents. He loved all sorts of animals and could care for them gently. He was also the producer of wonderful drawings, as was his friend, and many sheets with beautifully detailed pictures might be produced within a short space of time when the mood was on them. Ricardo specialized in trains, which were drawn with wheels, rails, smoke-stacks and so on. He was, however, not willing to enter into contact with practitioners, and it was not often that there was any access to his imaginative world.

When one day he was seen sitting with his friend at a table the member of staff in the room at the time thought it would be good to be nearby in case there was an opportunity to make contact. She observed unobtrusively, waiting for a suitable moment. Ricardo was playing with a puppet that he had made from scraps of felt the previous day. It was in the form of a long strip of green felt with stitches folding over enough material at one end to make a small triangular face and form a little pocket for two fingers to fit inside so the head could be moved about. It was called 'Snakey'; it was the first object Ricardo had created at school, and enormously precious to him. It was also precious to the practitioners because of the progress it represented. The day before, the same member of staff had managed to help him with it when he reached a difficult point and showed distress about it.

Ricardo was sitting on his own at a table with some dough, with Snakey on his left hand. He was making little balls of dough which he pressed onto a larger, disc-shaped, lump of dough. He was joined by Sunil, his friend, with whom he had a close but often stormy relationship. Sunil at first used a separate piece of dough but then tried to take dough from the big round that Ricardo was busy with. The result was screams, physical resistance and shouts of 'No, it's Snakey's'.

The practitioner walked over and asked 'Hello, what's going on? What is it?' and was told that it was Snakey's birthday cake. This gave the practitioner an opportunity to support and encourage some of Ricardo's pursuits, and the practitioner sat down (after asking if this was acceptable) to share in the making of the cake. Another first was achieved – the first time Ricardo had been known to share his interests with a member of staff. There were brief discussions of how the cake was made (by mixing and pounding, it seems from the gestures, and by putting in butter and chocolate drops, from Sunil's suggestion), of how many people would come (the three people who were present in this group at the table were pointed to) and of how old Snakey was and how many candles he would have (four, but the practitioner noted without comment that there were many more than four small balls representing candles on the cake).

After a while the cake-making ran out of ideas, and the practitioner suggested making a house for Snakey to have his birthday party in. Boxes were chosen and fetched by the boys, and Sunil was encouraged to make a house for his own Snakey – luckily he had made his own the day before. Ricardo quickly cut out a door shape in the box, confirmed that this was where Snakey went out and in, and followed this briefly with a few strokes of the brush. 'It's finished', he said. When asked what he would like to do next he said 'Make a bed for Snakey!' and chose a long thin box with one side in plastic so that the puppet could be seen lying inside. This was the end of the collaboration, and he turned to Sunil (who had been trying to get him to come outside for some time) and said 'Come on, let's go!'

The member of staff was left to reckon up the gains from this unexpected bonus. Ricardo had revealed a great deal more of his positive thoughts and feelings than ever before; he had shown interest in both creating and providing for Snakey, and had been showing that he was aware of how one might need to look after creatures one is responsible for. This was particularly significant in view of his very difficult home relationships and his behaviour to other children at school. He had used, although only briefly in two cases, three different ways of representing things in the dough, the boxes and the paint. He had shared his interests with a practitioner – this was most encouraging. He showed that he knew about the link between candles and age, although not on this occasion linking this with the lumps of dough – something which further observation would help to clarify. Passing out pieces of apple might be a good opportunity – one each for the boys and one for each puppet? He chose his boxes sensibly for his purpose and avoided doing any work on the bed by getting it in the right shape from the start. He was able, with practitioner help, to work collaboratively with Sunil.

The significance of the evidence about the development of Ricardo's attitude to himself and others was confirmed a day later when he was with Snakey in the book corner, shouting at others to go out because he was feeling squashed. A practitioner came with an offer to read a story to him and Snakey. He replied 'Snakey read a story!' He chose a book and sat with it on his knees so that Snakey could see to 'read' it. His voice was an almost inaudible whisper and the other children, who had been ready to accept this development, became restless because they could not hear. He reproved them with great teacher-like strictness: 'No! You – don't talk!' The practitioner was then able to suggest holding the book up so the others could see, and Ricardo beamed with pleasure at the children as he turned the pages, making gestures as one who retells a story and producing indistinct sounds like a story heard from very far away. Eventually he agreed to let Snakey finish the story on the hand of the practitioner, who conjectured that although he had chosen the book deliberately he either did not know the story well or was unready to retell it to a group.

This episode demonstrated another role that Ricardo was able to reproduce in his play activities – both the caring parent and the teacher were established in his mind. He was well aware of the use of books and although he could not reproduce the story from the pictures he knew which way the book needed to be for the puppet on his knee to read the words, and which way to hold it so that the other children could see the pictures. The fact that these understandings were able to be explored with practitioners and other children was of great significance for his future educational experiences. A child who might have a prospect of a career of educational disturbance and disruption in spite of his obvious gifts, had the chance to experience practitioners and other children as potential collaborators.

For the practitioners who were concerned with his progress it was an opportunity to make contact with his own purposes and pursuits so that education could offer something rather than oppose his interests. This made it particularly rewarding when, ten days later, he assumed the role of guardian of some ants he found in the playground and the practitioners were again able to encourage his concern for their welfare, which he expressed in a play scenario bearing close resemblances to a television action drama. 'Look how many ants I got!' 'How many?' (Considered ants, of which there were five, held up all the fingers of one hand starfish-wise, as younger children do, looked at them, curled them up again and then held up two fingers.) The member of staff asked 'Is that how many?' Ricardo nodded. 'It looks like more than that to me.' Ricardo was not interested in exact numbers. He fetched a lid for the container, screamed at some other children he feared would try to take his ants, then dropped the container. 'Hey, look at my ants dead!' He gathered them up again, and this time invited the others to see them. 'You wanna see my ants?' Children began to ask to see them and for some reason this provoked a wild charge around the playground as if the ants were in great danger. He and Sunil rushed into the classroom, where he opened the lid with care. 'My ants safe?' They went back out, rushed around again and then went into another classroom with the container of ants.

This episode might be seen as showing a scientific interest, and it is certainly important that the care of living creatures should be followed up and developed as a theme. Even more, though, there is a theme of protecting interests which applies both to the ants and to the possessor of them. However, some may have reservations about whether this sort of theme has any place in a discussion about how children learn. Is this topic too personal to the child to be considered educational material? Perhaps it is too personal, too closely bound up with Ricardo's own emotional development, to be a fit subject for members of staff to give priority to?

It seems more likely that this is an illustration of how the preoccupations of individual children give practitioners the chance to help with the development of positive attitudes to learning and to learning in groups, and also to create educational provision which reaches high standards within a focus that has already engaged children's interest. To enlist Ricardo's concern for small creatures within an investigation of life-forms and their needs would be to introduce him and the children who were inspired by him to natural science. He would also benefit from the chance to play out his ideas about practitioner roles and about institutions like school. This would help him understand the worlds of home and school better – as with his experience of reading to other children. Without being encouraged in his role-playing he might not understand enough about school, for instance, to get much benefit from it. If he could play at being a teacher he might build up ideas about teachers as people not too different from him, and this would help in his relationships with them. The same might be true about home. If he could play with ideas about what his mother was trying to do for him he might find it easier to get along with her efforts to bring him up. It is possible that his care for Snakey and for the ants was related to ideas about looking after dependent creatures. This might link up with his ideas about his mother as someone who cared for him.

The development of children's minds is a subject which can be approached through thinking about the meaning and implications of their play, investigations and talk. It is a subject on which much has been written and where practitioner understanding at a theoretical level is deepening all the time. This understanding is the basis on which we build, and the framework into which we fit what we learn from the children with whom we have contact; from these observations, incidental and planned, we see minds growing through making their own internal models of the world and through exploring these models with other children and with practitioners. Growing minds are both active and collaborative; they need to make their own ideas about the world and to have practitioners with whom to extend their understanding.

Four-year-olds in reception classes

The foregoing discussion has outlined the general principles which should underpin educational provision in early childhood. The fact that the great majority of the nation's four-year-olds are in reception classes in infant or primary schools gives acute cause for concern. Provision for them should take account of their extreme youth; there must be few, if any, other nations which would require children of this age to learn according to the practices of the compulsory sector of education.

These children are at an age where they need the staff ratios, resources and curriculum approach outlined here; it is essential that they be in classes where nursery conditions and requirements apply and in the care of nursery trained staff. Their status as nursery-age children should not be compromised by the administrative convenience of making room for them in reception classes; education is not at any age about administrative convenience, but about providing appropriate educational experiences for the learner.

A curriculum appropriate to their needs is necessary for all children's learning. For children like Ricardo, the lack of such a curriculum could deny him a chance of successful learning later. Moreover, it is not the under-fives alone who need this kind of curriculum; children between five and seven or eight also learn in the ways outlined here. The early childhood approach to the curriculum is strongly supported by recent research (see, e.g. Wells, 1987; Bruner and Haste, 1987) and has been accepted as the right approach for the youngest children in compulsory school by government-appointed bodies from the Hadow Committee (Board of Education, 1931) onwards. International comparisons confirm this view in that most other developed nations not only begin compulsory schooling at a later date than does the UK but also provide for their under-sixes or under-sevens a sound framework of nursery education which takes as read their right to provision related to their developmental needs (see, e.g. Woodhead, 1986, 1989). In this country, because of the way that compulsory education cuts across the age-group, nursery and infant education are divided from each other although they should be seen together in continuous alignment with the developmental needs of the child. It is in the interests of four-year-olds for the early years curriculum to be seen as the context for provision for them, within which the needs of children of their age are best met in nursery conditions, just as it is in the interests of all children under seven or eight for their educational experiences to be seen in the context of the early years curriculum in the infant or first school.

Conclusion

It is vital that the implementation of any curriculum requirements should be based upon an informed understanding of the need for continuity with the early childhood curriculum; the under-fives, as nursery-age children caught up in the requirements of the compulsory sector, will be by far the worst affected if this does not happen, but older children will also experience lack of continuity at a time when they are making the vital transition to the world of school. This transition takes place over the early years of education and requires positive action to support children with provision appropriate to this vulnerable stage. The introduction of the National Curriculum has taken attention away from the developmental needs of young children; its review, as practitioners begin to evaluate its effects, presents an opportunity to address the issues of the needs of the very youngest children in school, and to try to ensure that provision for them draws on the strengths of the early childhood curriculum.

Further reading

Gura, P. (ed.) (1992) *Exploring Learning: Young Children and Block-play*, Paul Chapman, London.

For discussion

After reading in Gura (1992) of the range of learning and expressing that takes place in blockplay, you will find it interesting to observe young children and blocks. It may help you to be aware of the decisions and problems they encounter if you explore blocks yourself.

Take a set of blocks, the biggest and the most well-made that you can find, and add to it some extra resources such as toy animals or people. Explore some of the different things that you personally can do with the blocks and toys, making interesting shapes, building stories, creating characters and so on. With a partner, and with one other person observing and making notes, decide what you both want to do with the blocks (you don't have to 'make' something representational). At the end of 15 minutes, ask the observer to tell you what aspects of the curriculum requirements for your work have been touched on; this could be the National Curriculum, Desirable Outcomes, HMI Areas of Experience, areas of development (social, emotional, physical, communicative, cognitive), Montessori, Steiner or High/Scope requirements. Talk through how well you feel the observer has noted what you were trying to do, and how well what the observer noted fits your experience of the blocks. Make notes of what other resources you would like to have available to carry your plans further.

3

What Do We Mean by Play?

So much has been said and written about play that it is difficult to imagine that valid new contributions to the debate are possible. Yet, in spite of all the research and the publications, we have not yet arrived at an understanding of children's own learning strategies and, in particular, their self-chosen playful activities. We very much need such an understanding to guide us in how we can best support and extend their achievements. Adults generally use the word 'play' to signify time away from work; we forget how, as babies and young children, we struggled to make sense of the world and our own place in it through our own strategies, especially imaginative and fantasy play. Our recollections from later schooldays of being told that work must be completed before we can enjoy time to play are much clearer than our memories of our earlier intense and effortful learning through play. The misunderstandings of young children's learning have been made worse by the way in which the National Curriculum introduced by the 1988 Education Reform Act was defined on the basis of the subject disciplines which form the secondary school curriculum. The requirements imposed on infant teachers by Key Stage 1 are subject-based with the exception of personal and social education and some concessions to occasional cross-curricular work; they make at most one or two references to play. The requirements placed on settings for children under five, the Desirable Outcomes for Children's Learning on Entry to Compulsory Schooling, aim to ensure that they prepare children for a subject-based approach. This development has been understood to mean that playful approaches to learning in the early years are now to come to an end (Blenkin and Kelly, 1994).

However, this is not how good provision for early learning is understood by the majority of practitioners. Findings from two major research and development projects, *Principles into Practice*

(Blenkin *et al.*, 1995) and *Quality in Diversity* (ECEF, 1997), show that those who work in the maintained, private and voluntary sectors are agreed that play, along with other developmentally-appropriate strategies for learning in the early years, is essential to the early years curriculum. For this reason, we need to go on trying to find out how young children's natural learning strategies should shape effective approaches to the curriculum in the early years. The main thrust of the effort will tend to be through defining the role of self-chosen play activities, because it is around this particular learning strategy that the arguments have been the most intense. How it is to be defined, and how more articulate definitions may help to improve practice, will depend on the understanding and commitment of early years practitioners.

Unfortunately, the role of play in early learning is not always easy for practitioners to define. Play can be physical, developing relationships as well as strength and skill. It can be sensory and exploratory, extending experience and through this developing understanding of the physical world. It can be creative, exploring and communicating feelings and representing thoughts. It can be imaginative and symbolic, enabling the players to develop their ideas and skills. All kinds of play can help children to develop their understanding of other people and their skills in collaborating with them. But is this an argument for providing for play in settings outside the home?

One of the main characteristics of play that makes it attractive to educators is the opportunities it presents for learning about very serious, even dangerous, matters in a risk-free way. The child is able to approach the real world with a 'standing-off' relationship with the risks attendant on reality; she or he can throw the baby out of the window, be a doctor cutting open someone's chest, engage in burglary, get married, and learn important things about these roles while risking no penalties for failure. It seems important that play should, in this way, free children from constraints of reality and of adult expectation. We can expect, in fact, that if play has these functions it would require an inner logic which would often be difficult for adults to share. As I shall suggest later on, children's processes in play may not always be opaque, and specific instances often give sensitive adults the chance to share in children's play, but the adult has to surrender the leadership role in order to become a collaborator.

Interpreting play

Among the many attempts by adults to find a perspective from which to view play, two broad approaches seem to exist. One tries to find ways to evaluate play in terms of measurement of the results – an instance of which would be the overview of research provided by Smith (1988). He contrasts the 'play ethos' with the disappointing results as measured by tightly-controlled experimental studies. He also finds it difficult to justify the 'play-tutoring' programmes as more effective than 'skills-tutoring' programmmes in promoting competence. He suggests that there are three possible explanations for his conclusions; that wrong procedures have been used, that the wrong outcomes have been measured or that

> the theoretical framework behind the 'play ethos' is, in part at least, incorrect . . . [and that we need to examine more exactly the type of play referred to, the context and structure, and how much time is spent] . . . Possibilities such as these do not amount to a reversal of the 'play ethos', but they do amount to a substantial re-evaluation. Second, they would suggest that we qualify hypothesized links in terms of what kinds of play, in what context, and for what periods of time. A next generation of play research might move to consider some of these questions, in so far as educational goals of play are sought.
>
> (Smith, 1988, pp. 221–3)

Another approach would be the view taken by Sponseller (1982), in which she draws attention to the difficulty that both naturalistic and experimental studies have in coming to grips with the subject, and suggests that we attend to our own problems in constructing appropriate theories and methods of enquiry. Teachers, in particular, should look to what they need to know about play and learn how to monitor the effect on children of what they do.

> For teachers, the significance of research on play is that it allows them to adopt an organising schema through which to view children's play. The meaningfulness of this research for teachers is its potential to assist them in forming their own questions about the play of the children they teach.
>
> Teachers may be unsure of how play research will affect their day-to-day classroom behaviour. Because of definitional problems, methodological problems, and the fact that reported results often conflict or lack clarity, teachers may feel that play research has little practical meaning. To translate research into practice, teachers need to decide on their goals for play facilitation: the types of play they wish to encourage and the developmental and/

or learning processes they wish to influence. They also need to become researchers themselves in the sense that they should monitor the effect on children of whatever tactic they implement.

(Sponseller, 1982, p. 231)

To carry out these suggestions – that what we should do is to look at our explorations of play more questioningly – we can follow up the idea of teachers researching the play in their own classrooms. A good standpoint for a discussion of play is the investigation of play as it appears in the behaviour of children that one is working with. The meaning that play appears to have in their lives will be an important element to consider in evaluating what its educational and developmental value might be.

Observing play

Close observation of play suggests that for those who are willing to try to learn there are illuminating insights into the ways in which children make sense not only of the world around them but also of their own experiences in it. The person who is sufficiently open-minded to be guided by children will be able to see children exercising control over their world through play. In this section we focus in greater depth upon some aspects of the dynamic force and creativity of play. In play, young children explore their world, take on roles in it, experiment with changing it, and represent their understanding of it as a world shared with others who have their own ideas and purposes. For the practitioner, there are opportunities to learn about how the children see the world around them, and what stage their understanding is at. As will be seen later, there are also valuable opportunities to structure play settings in such a way as to take advantage of children's strong motivation to learn through engaging their feelings, interests and imagination in a play scenario.

Play and the 'as if' mode

I wish here to offer a personal view of ways in which learning about the world and the self in early childhood can take shape in play. This view is largely based on observation of children playing at home, in school and in museum provision.

I believe that learning is largely dependent on play for the mental models of the world which constitute its internalization in the

early years. These models can only be constructed in a hypotheti-
cal, 'as if it were', or 'what if it were', mode which Guha (1996)
describes. Through this mode children are able to manipulate
aspects of the world they are familiar with and develop their
understanding and work out appropriate responses.

This process extends to the appreciation of aspects of real and
very close situations. The instance Vygotsky (1966) gives of siblings actually playing at being siblings is one that I have observed
myself, and it illustrates for me how much children need to play in
order to come to terms with their reality. My own children, when
of nursery and infant school age, used to construct play situations
of this kind. One would initiate with 'Let's pretend we were sisters'
and the other would usually extend the proposal in some way,
such as (with a forthrightness quite startling to the parent) 'Yes,
and our Mummy and Daddy were dead.' This led to hours of play
around the idea of siblings caring for each other and co-operating
in a context of mutual dependence.

Paul Harris (1990) describes his perspective on play and the
development of understanding of emotion in terms of its being 'a
key that unlocks the minds of other people and allows the child to
enter temporarily into their plans, hopes and fears' (pp. 18–19).
This search for a key to unlock the minds of other people can be
seen particularly clearly when children are dealing with very difficult aspects of adult behaviour.

Social relationships and play

In observing this process I believe that we are seeing children
trying to understand and come to terms with the interactions they
experience daily. It is also the key to the way some individual
children attempt to surmount difficulties in relationships. In order
to look in depth at this process I will give one example. It is the
suitability of play for such vital purposes, as well as children's
inclination to seek it whenever possible, which ought to make an
impression on those who care for them.

Jeanette

Jeanette was under three when she started school; she was offered
a place as a matter of urgency because both she and her older sister
had been subjected to abuse by their parents. She displayed

complete independence from her first day, with no apparent need to make contact with her mother or with any other adult; there was a continued detachment from adults in the classroom, but within a very short time she revealed a great purpose and mature sociability in play with her peers. This very small and frail-looking child piled much larger and older children into the old wooden pram and heaved them lovingly around the playground, mothering them continuously with the imaginary meals, bedtimes, outings and birthday parties we are all familiar with. Anyone in tears drew her attention at once.

The most striking example of her caring was associated with another child's unhappiness which she tried to resolve through imaginative play around her own concerns. It took place during a story session I had set up with the youngest in the class when she took on the care of a newly entered boy almost twice her size who suddenly became tired and tearful as home-time approached. She scooped him up and hauled him onto her knees as they sat together on the carpet; she hugged him, jogged him on her knees and told him not to cry. Following this she instituted with him under my startled gaze – to the great distraction and delight of the other four children – an enthralling game. She laid her finger on her lips, and raised her eyebrows as high as they would go while fixing his eyes with hers – the 'imaginary play' face which we often use to indicate a dramatic scenario – and then directed his gaze to a closed door near where we were sitting through which could be heard sounds of dinner being prepared. She drew in her breath sharply – a technique of storytellers to communicate excitement – and said; 'Don't go through there! There's witches in there . . . Are you frightened?'

From that moment my story was lost, and we had entered a world akin to the fairy-tale resolution of life's problems noted by Bettelheim (1975).

> The fairy story begins where the child is at this time in his life and where, without the help of the story, he would remain stuck: feeling neglected, rejected, downgraded. Then, using thought processes which are his own – contrary to adult rationality as these may be – the story opens glorious vistas which permit the child to overcome momentary feelings of utter hopelessness. In order to believe the story, and to make its optimistic outlook part of his world experience, the child needs to hear it many times. If in addition he acts it out, this makes it that much more 'true' and 'real'.
>
> The child feels which of the many fairy tales is true to his inner situation of the moment (which he is unable to deal with on his

own), and he also feels where the story provides him with a handle for coming to grips with a difficult problem.

(Bettelheim, 1975, p. 58)

If fairy tales fulfil the role that Bettelheim assigns to them in the successful psychic overcoming of life problems, then it seems likely that they do this through being imaginative models of the world in which to explore the playful resolution of dilemmas along lines that have been found to be successful by earlier generations. In the same way, Jeanette adopted the fairy tale mode to express and deal with the existence of powerful unfriendly forces in her own environment by constructing a picture of them as external to her own world of experience, but contingent to it and capable of impinging on it if one did something foolish like going through the wrong door.

I am struck now, reflecting on my time observing her, with how all of a piece her behaviour was with this imaginary scenario. In the classroom and playground she avoided contact with the giants and witches who roamed dangerously around, and created a safe and self-contained world of caring around her peers, many of whom found her a stimulating and warm presence especially in their early days. Some of her most successful games of parenthood were with Luke, a few months older than her, whose mother had left the family shortly after the birth of his younger sister. I have a photograph of Jeanette and Luke wheeling the old pram in the playground, Jeanette pushing and Luke walking along beside with his hand on the sleeve of her coat. From the few snatches of conversation that I overheard I feel fairly certain that Jeanette's mothering was enabling him to be a big boy helping with the pram and the shopping. Jeanette's self-healing could be a positive force for him, too.

This kind of play about family and other social relationships is extremely common in all settings and easily seen wherever there is a child and another participant, whether living or a toy of some kind. In their play about human relationships children explore both the behaviour of other people and the possibilities for their own roles and actions. There does not have to be a gross injury for this to take place, and in fact it is likely that when children do have a very serious problem in their lives it will be more, not less, difficult for them to play.

In the case of a preschool setting, an appropriate early years curriculum, a well-planned learning environment and an adult role based on supporting and extending children's social and emotional development could be expected to give children the understanding and support they need. But do adults in compulsory education need to do more than provide a safe setting for play? Is play any more than a way of coming to terms with human relationships? Does it have a role in the kind of learning that we wish children to do about other aspects of the world, the kind of learning that we expect to go on in school? Is there a difference between play in general and 'play in school' (Guha, 1996), and what do practitioners need to do to provide the latter?

Play and education

Many practitioners, and teachers among them, are committed to the importance of play yet often uncertain about the place of play in the classroom. Cleave, Jowett and Bate (1982) found that primary teachers tended to see play as opposed to work, and Sestini (1987) has pointed out that four-year-olds in the infant school may themselves seem to accept a view of school that excludes play. Cleave and Brown (1989) have found that while play is seen as 'the basis of other activities' and 'an experiential activity-based approach through which the child makes sense of the world' (Cleave and Brown, 1989, p. 51) there are problems for teachers in demonstrating the contribution that play makes to children's progress. This may lead to a lack of confidence in what is being achieved, and to an unconscious tendency to dismiss what happens in the home corner or sand tray as less valuable than such activities as reading and writing (ibid., p. 52). Each of these studies adds to the picture of practitioners' uncertainty about whether, and if so how, play can make a contribution to formal learning as well as to children's emotional and social development. It also appears, perhaps as a result of these uncertainties, that there are gaps between the theories held by practitioners and their actual practice. Bennett, Wood and Rogers (1997) report in their study of teachers' beliefs and practice that, 'in general, play was far more structured in practice than teachers' theoretical accounts indicated.' They also found that there were many occasions on which teachers' adherence in theory to children's freedom to choose the subject of their play was in conflict with the need for a more active adult share in the play if the teacher's intentions were to be achieved (ibid., p. 75). This issue of the role of the adult in 'play in school' will be dealt with in greater detail in the next section of this chapter.

The question is whether the outstanding characteristics of play noted above apply to cognitive, discipline-based learning as well as to understanding of human emotion. The present concentration on the requirements of the National Curriculum tends towards a focus on the direct teaching of skills and knowledge. Is there room for an awareness of what play can offer to children as pupils through extending their understanding of the meaning, value and usefulness of these skills and this knowledge?

Some would say not, and that the developmental approach to education has been responsible for a lack of intellectual force in classroom provision. The focus on subject-based learning in the National Curriculum documents adds to the impression that play is seen as separate from the high quality learning that is aimed for. Yet it is possible that without the learning opportunities offered by play the aims of the National Curriculum will not be achieved.

Learning through play in museums

As well as the capacity for imaginative projection into human situations and predicaments, young children bring to the process of learning their capacity for active involvement with materials, for representation of their experiences, and for the exploration of experience through spontaneous play. Experimental provision at the National Maritime Museum in 1988 (the Armada Exhibition) offered opportunities to engage with historical ideas and knowledge in various ways within a planned learning environment constructed as a galleon wrecked on a Scottish shore: historically appropriate dressing-up clothes and foodstuffs were available, there were materials for drawing and painting on hand, and play with miniature world and construction materials was encouraged. We were hopeful that play would occur, but not at all sure what kind of play would be observed. In fact, it became clear that play was taking place and that, with adult support and interaction, children were coming to grips with important themes of the exhibition.

1. *Miniature world play:* the students had prepared a table-top to be a seascape with groups of islands (blue paper for the

sea and crumpled brown paper for islands). There were small boats of various shapes and sizes, and a number of people to ride in them. There were additional materials for children to use if they wished to develop the scene. A boy of five and a boy of seven sat down with their mother, who remained quietly supportive and aware of their play throughout the fifteen minutes or so of the episode. The older boy played by himself in silence, using paper and glue to make more islands, while the younger one moved the people and boats according to his own dramatic play scenario, imagining scenes of wreck, dying, hiding in caves, swimming to the shore, sailing to pick up survivors and massacre by 'baddies'. He was very willing to express his ideas in conversation, and was not ready to leave when the session was over.

2. *Imaginative construction play*: four children (three girls and a boy) between the ages of three and six, were playing on the floor with a small wooden construction kit. This included cylinders which could rotate if a thin stick was inserted into a hole to act as an axis. Themes which they explored in their building and in their conversation with me were to do with rotating, linked with turning a cannon, with levers, linked with machinery on the ship such as the pump, wheels, linked with steering, height, (somewhere for a look-out to sit), size, (the biggest ship, the most number of people on it), and enclosed spaces, related to different rooms and different uses for them on the ship.

3. *Domestic play*: a child of 22 months was observed 'making dinner' in the forecastle; Tom used a wooden spoon to ladle imaginary food from one of the big casks into a wooden bowl, saying as he did so in response to my talk, 'ninna', that we were having beans and 'tatoes', and offering 'more'. He was unable to associate the water-sack with drink, but used the more familiar utensils with a clear sense of their meaning, in a way that illustrates how deep the importance of actual artefacts goes in children's take-up of educational provision, and suggests that domestic-type play should be a prominent feature of future development.

The *Bounty* exhibition which followed in 1989 provided similar opportunities. In particular, I noted a group of four girls between the ages of about six and eleven or so playing an extended game of creeping around the ship to steal 'the provisions' while the captain was briefly away, in the course of which they seemed to be dealing with ideas about authority (and perhaps the personality of Bligh himself), about the life and death seriousness of stealing food on a ship, and about the kind of provisions they might find there. Two younger children aged three and four, having been introduced to the sacks, casks and barrels of food and drink, asked where they would have been cooked. If a replica stove had been available they too could have found a way to make the salt fish, pulses, sauerkraut and so on a part of their understanding.

Some findings from museum work; play and learning

Perhaps the most challenging issue which confronts practitioners who teach young children is how to try to reconcile children's developmental needs with their need to learn about the world around them. Belief in the importance of play does not excuse us from energetically and thoughtfully pursuing the education of our children – rather it helps by giving us guidelines for how best to proceed.

Practitioners have at present to deal with the demands of a subject-based curriculum; it seems to be here that the adult world, with its separation of subject disciplines for educational purposes, is most at odds with the holistic and unitary thinking of the young child and in fact with the way the world works as well.

A full theoretical exploration of the nature of the young child's conceptual approaches and strategies towards the surrounding world would be out of place here, but it is helpful to look at the Science Museum's approach to starting science. 'The Garden', the gallery for children of preschool and infant age, has been planned to build on the contrast between the adult's concerns to teach about the physical aspects of science and technology and the children's existing ideas about what is being offered. The Museum staff have provided activities and experiences within the context of children's developmental learning strategies – exploration, communication, stories and play (Graham, 1995).

As practitioners we know that we have to relate the experiences and activities provided to the children's pre-existing understandings and to their developmental learning potential. To provide for play is the only way in which to begin this process, and to observe and respond to the play is the only way to continue it. Practitioners and parents are fortunate in that they know children over long periods of time, and have the opportunity to observe and reflect upon their play.

Play and learning about the world

In play children are encountering facts and ideas about the world and ways of expressing this thinking, and facts and ideas about the way human life is organized in roles and relationships. Many instances could be quoted of young children's exploration through play of what it means to be the driver of the bus, the cook, the deliverer of bricks, of milk or letters. However it is also possible to understand more clearly the learning potential of the play of young children if we see it as a part of a continuum of learning which extends into older age-groups and can take place in other educational settings as well as in schools. If children are to learn effectively about the world they need to re-create and re-work experience in play. From studies across the primary years and into secondary education we learn that, if children are to be able to use the opportunity of play in school to learn about the world, they need the active participation and support of practitioners. In play children evoke particular situations or roles and interpret their reality in a very active way. This appears to involve an internalization and creative representation of reality in which children are achieving an increased capacity to handle real situations; the representation of reality by Year 8 classes studying democracy and dictatorship in ancient Rome is dependent on intense activity by the practitioner (Towill, 1997), as are the younger children in the Science Museum.

From the examples given it seems likely that this learning comes about through each child building up a personal construction, an imaginative model, of the situation in question *on the basis of the information given*. With regard to the acquisition of understanding, knowledge and skills, whether of formal academic learning or of social and emotional relationships, it cannot be right to downgrade the role of the adult in providing a carefully thought out structure for the learning, both in advance and through active, and sensitive, participation in the play. For the child this can lead not only to the solution of a problem or the resolution of a particular dilemma, but also to a new way of experiencing an aspect of the world. This is the child's active and unique way of coming to terms with the world and with others' experience of it as well. The efforts of very young children to understand the world through encountering it in play are unique and irreplaceable.

In relation to practitioners' responsibilities under the National Curriculum and the Desirable Outcomes the principle to draw from this is that we must negotiate with children about their learning on the basis of our own knowledge of their present understanding and the appropriate next steps for them. We must assess children's levels of understanding and interests through observation and record-keeping, and must use our assessments to enable us to plan appropriate educational experiences. We have to be the mediators between the bodies of knowledge that are thought important for children to have access to, and the children's own developing ideas about the world.

Lastly, play is a safe way in which to learn the realities of the world. For adults, play modes are used to explore possibilities without incurring the penalties of implementation; architects make scale drawings and models, representing mental models of interactions and procedures – a process that might be called imaging. Children learning about the feudal system play out their roles from briefs that help them to make mental models of other times; in real life it would take many years to acquire understanding of the role of the medieval bailiff in the feudal system. In play, the information can become real much more quickly.

1. Along with everyone else, you must address the lord properly, as 'my Lord'. You must apologise even if you are not wrong.
2. You can take out your hatred on the serf – call him/her 'serf' in a nasty way, for instance. S/he must call you 'sir' – if s/he forgets then remind him/her of his/her place in life.

(Towill, 1997, p. 11)

In imagining themselves into situations and possibilities, adults also, like children, project their internal models onto the world in a range of ways, the most powerful of which resemble children's play in important, and, I would suggest, connected aspects. Children's play links with the ways in which all humans, adults as well, come to make personal sense of the world.

Play in consequence belongs, with the processes of exploration and representation, at the centre of our picture of the learning process of all humans. Susan Isaacs (1929) draws our attention to the biological perspective, in which the greater the degree of play in any species of mammal, the higher the level of learning by the individual.

> If now we compare again the more adaptable and intelligent animals with the less, for instance, the reptiles and fishes with the mammals, we notice something which throws much light on human childhood – viz: the fact that the animals which are able to learn more are also able to play more. Those with fixed and inherited instincts play not at all; the young behave as the old from the beginning, and there is nothing to add to the wisdom of the species. But the playing animals, and in proportion as they play, gain something of an individual wisdom. They are the curious, the experimental animals. The young lamb skips, but only for a short time, and soon settles down into sheep-like stolidity. Whereas the kitten plays on, and tries its way about the world with playful paw and nose, long after its age and size might lead us to expect a sober maturity. Those animals nearest to ourselves, the monkey and the ape, are like us in keeping the will to play even into maturity; but no animal young play so freely, so inventively, so continually and so long as human children.
>   All this would suggest that play means much as a way of development for the learning animal; and those who have watched the play of children have long looked upon it as Nature's means of individual education.
>
>   (Isaacs, 1929, p. 9)

Conclusion

This section presents a personal view of play which looks at ways in which learning about the world and the self in early childhood takes shape in play. I believe play has a doubly important role in learning. Firstly, effective educational play activities help children acquire the understanding, information and skills they need in a user-friendly way which protects them against stress and uncertainty. This process has links with the ways in which all humans, adults as well, come to make personal sense of the world. Secondly, as practitioners we see in young children's play, their physical activity and talk, the evidence of how they are arranging experiences in their minds in an 'as if' or 'what if' mode, and this gives us the information we need to teach them more and better.

Further reading

Goldschmied, E. and Jackson, S. (1994) *People Under Three: Young Children in Day Care*, Routledge, London. See in particular pp. 7–9 on the importance of play, and the sections on Treasure Basket and Heuristic Play.

Graham, J. (1995) *The Garden*, Trustees of the Science Museum, London.

For discussion

From your reading and from your own experiences, what are the criteria for play which benefit children? In particular, what should practitioners and parents do to support play?

Different kinds of play are noted in this chapter, including Jeanette's self-healing fantasies and her play with other children whose emotional needs she sympathized with. Is provision for this kind of play in educational settings a luxury? If not, how do we justify it in educational terms?

4

Understanding the Curriculum

Much has been written about the curriculum and here we will not go in depth into the arguments about curriculum theory; a discussion of the issues will be found elsewhere in Kelly, 1990, Blenkin and Kelly (1981), Kelly (1986) and Blyth (1984). Summing up the issue, Kelly proposes that those who engage in curriculum development or innovation need to be aware of the choices that are there to be made, and should be prepared to justify the decisions that they have taken.

> There are several important respects in which our understanding of the complexities of curriculum planning and development has been extended in recent years. It has become apparent, for example, both from the experience of those who have been engaged in curriculum innovation and from reflection upon their experience, that one can adopt several quite distinct approaches towards curriculum planning and that, as a result of this kind of insight, due attention must be paid by the curriculum planner to the selection of the approach appropriate to his or her purposes . . . It will be apparent, therefore, that any exercise in curriculum planning, from that of the individual teacher to that of the national planner, must take account of these understandings and certainly must be evaluated against the perspectives they offer. Strictly, such planning should include explanations of how it has taken such account and/or why it has chosen its particular model or approach, so that its thinking can be evaluated in the light of such explanations.
>
> (Kelly, 1990, pp. 57–8)

Different approaches to the curriculum

Among the different curriculum approaches to which Kelly refers is the early years curriculum. This has been acknowledged since at least the 1920s (see, for instance, Isaacs, 1929, and the Hadow Committee's definition, Board of Education, 1931). It is a concept of the curriculum in early childhood which has influenced generation after generation of practitioners and been developed by them in their turn. In spite of the National Curriculum's definition of subject areas to be taught and the different levels of achievement, the practitioner working with children under the age of eight still has, therefore, very important decisions to take. The early years curriculum is based on statements of principle which arise from a shared value-base giving high priority to what is now called developmentally appropriate practice (Bredekamp, 1987) in supporting children's own learning strategies. It has been described and defined by groups of practitioners in almost every local education authority in England and Wales, by large groups such as the Early Childhood Education Forum (1997) and by small groups such as the Early Years Curriculum Group (1989, 1992). It has been analysed by individual writers and writing teams such as Blenkin and Kelly (1981, 1996), Bruce (1987, 1991), and Whitebread (1996). It differs from the National Curriculum and the Desirable Outcomes in basing its criteria of quality on underlying principles based on how young children learn, rather than on definitions of outcomes in terms of knowledge and skills acquired by children. The Early Years Curriculum Group has shown how principles can be used to interpret the National Curriculum's requirements (forthcoming, 1998).

The early years curriculum has not been lacking in rigorous and challenging experiences for children; indeed, the Early Years Curriculum Group (1989) has demonstrated how good practice in the years before five can show achievements according to the National Curriculum long before children are of an age to be subject to it. There is also a growing list of practitioner reflections on the curriculum for children between birth and three, many using video to support their assertions. These show how younger children can be challenged in a similar way to learn about themselves, the people nearest to them and the world around (Goldschmied and Jackson, 1994; Goldschmied and Selleck, 1996; Early Childhood Education Forum, 1997).

However, there are points where the early years curriculum's tradition of developmentally appropriate provision for learning bring it sharply into conflict with current requirements to show children's gains in learning according to performance criteria. Baseline assessment brings this conflict into prominence as does assessment at Key Stage 1. Children's development has its own pace in each individual, and the age at which certain benchmarks in formal performance are reached can vary greatly. All children cannot achieve the same minimum level of performance in formal operations at this early age. Aims such as these are not considered to be appropriate for children between the ages of five and seven in most other countries. It is not that these aims are too high for most children, but rather that both the performance and the formal elements are unsuitable for children whose learning is still very personal and informal.

There are also, however, areas of the early years curriculum which themselves demand development, and this and the following chapters of this book are dedicated to setting out some immediate, practical ways in which practitioners can tackle these gaps.

Developing the early years curriculum

In general terms, these gaps are not so much serious weaknesses as areas remaining to be filled in through analysis of practice. They arise because the early years curriculum is based on statements of principle which have left it to the individual practitioner to put the principles into practice and to decide how successfully the aims have been achieved. For example, the previous chapter has set out some of the issues that surround provision for play in schools. Drummond (1989) fears that there is a conceptual gap underlying the general consensus among practitioners on the value of play as a teaching and learning strategy and the aims for learning in early childhood which support this view. Bennett, Wood and Rogers (1997) believe that what they call the 'play ideology' to which practitioners refer for justification of play in education is inadequate to support good practice, and they demonstrate how practice and principle differ in individual teachers they observed; they may well be right in saying that a more rigorous self-criticism based on classroom research is needed, although what kind of research is best needs to be debated.

These gaps can be filled in where practitioners are well-supported in ways which maintain and increase their expertise rather than undermining and disempowering them. Experience of action-research approaches confirms this (Kelly and Rose, 1996). For those who are feeling uncertain of their principles and unsupported in their practice in today's challenging world, however, such gaps are very dangerous. They are particularly so because there is an alternative model of learning achievement in young children which is available to parents and others who have a right to expect much from education in early childhood. This model is a simple one, and its apparent simplicity makes it the more acceptable, and its similarity to the reduced curriculum of the late nineteenth century elementary school (Blenkin and Kelly, 1994) gives it a traditional ring which is reassuring for those who fear change. Its definition of early childhood education is one which diminishes the power and value of young children as learners, and consigns them and their practitioners to the bottom of the curriculum heap with 'basic skills' and watered-down versions of the curriculum for older children. Anyone who doubts the official weight behind this approach should note the invitation given by Gillian Shephard as Secretary of State for Education and Employment to members of the Early Childhood Education Forum to endorse her definition of preschool education as concerned with 'numbers, colours, letters and doing up shoelaces' (pers. comm. 1995). The battle over what should be included in the Desirable Outcomes was largely fought behind the scenes at the DfEE during a protracted period of drafting in 1995 and 1996, in which comments and drafts received from practitioners and early years organizations pushed drafts towards the developmental approach and central government pulled them back towards the performance-based approach. The final version (SCAA) represents an uncomfortable compromise in which, for instance, children on the one hand (with appropriate allowance for developmental variations) 'use a growing vocabulary with increasing fluency to express thoughts and convey meaning', while on the other hand there is a clear expectation of performance in formal learning previously associated with infant schooling in 'They recognise letters of the alphabet by shape and sound' (SCAA, 1996, p. 10).

Negotiation between developmental principles and these curriculum requirements demands considerable expertise and self-confidence in practitioners. The way forward identified in this book aims to improve early years expertise and to demonstrate its value. It is based on the understanding that both the quality of early childhood education and its justification lie in the scrupulously accurate record-keeping of the practitioner. It is not a new suggestion; it owes much to the methods of Isaacs (1929). In recent times it has been stated over and over again by experienced practitioners such as Edgington (forthcoming 1998), and justified theoretically by work such as that of Athey (1990). An example is analysed below (Figure 4.1) to show how the bridges can be built

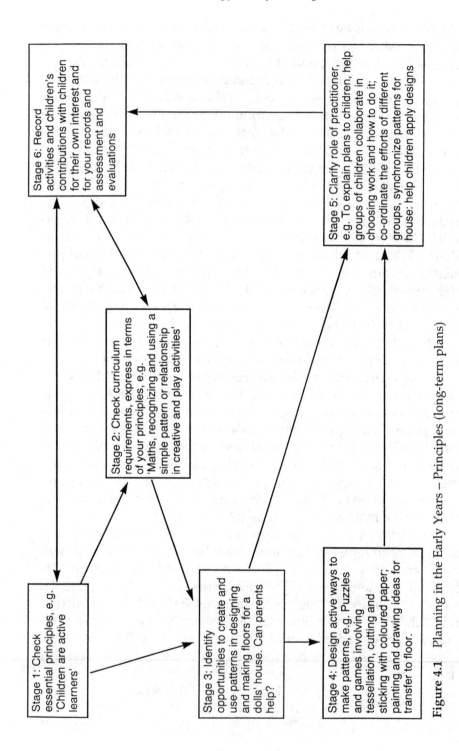

Figure 4.1   Planning in the Early Years – Principles (long-term plans)

between the developmentally appropriate early years curriculum and the performance-oriented requirements of central government. These bridges enable practitioners to make decisions about providing for children's learning in the knowledge that although there are different ideas about what a curriculum is, the ultimate aim of all is well-founded learning. If this can be demonstrated to be taking place, the dilemmas over the curriculum become less acute, because the more exact knowledge of how children are progressing and what best facilitates this progress will enable decisions to be made on a sound basis.

Practitioners will still have to consider how they see the curriculum; whether it is a statement about the knowledge to be learned, or the pupil behaviour sought, or whether it is perhaps a description of the process which goes on at school in which case it is not purely about adult intentions but also about pupil experience as well. They will, however, be able to reassure themselves and others that their decisions are based on good evidence drawn from careful observation.

One of the most important ways in which these decisions can be evaluated and subjected to a professional critique is in the examination of the quality of knowledge and understanding that children are acquiring. This chapter will show how careful monitoring of children's progress can reassure parents and practitioners that children can achieve according to the relevant curriculum requirements without any sacrifice of developmental principle.

Knowledge and the early years curriculum

I believe that the way that the early years curriculum approaches the teaching of knowledge about the world is closer by far than is any other curriculum to the way that human beings need to acquire that knowledge and the understanding that it serves. It is also closer to the processes through which human beings have explored and categorized the world throughout history in that it is built up through personal experience and interaction leading to the development of understanding. This process differs very much from the advance determination of what is to be known and understood, yet, contrary to claims that it allows lower standards to be set, it challenges the learner to take far greater responsibility for learning.

I believe that it also places a great responsibility on the adult, but that this is no greater a burden than that of any committed teacher and that it in fact makes the practitioner's task easier, not more difficult. While the early years curriculum applies to the entire age-range from birth to eight, now that the infant curriculum has been redefined as Key Stage 1 of the National Curriculum the nursery curriculum is the clearest example of a developmental early years curriculum and its benefits to children, parents and practitioners. Many of its principles and approaches form the basis of the developmental approach to infant education (Blenkin and Kelly, 1981, 1996). The following section explores what it has to show about developmental approaches and the quality of children's learning.

Examining the nursery curriculum

It is vital to understand the nursery curriculum as a whole before examining a part of it. When setting out to explore the nursery curriculum we have to look at it from two angles: it is both a provision for the the youngest children in school and the educational foundation for later learning. The principles of the provision are more important than the details of any one example, and it is the nursery approach that is being described rather than a blueprint for precise reproduction.

The curriculum in nursery schools and classes has always been described as founded on understandings and insights both about very young children and about how human beings learn in general. Knowledge about the nature of the learning process and about the particular needs of pupils of a particular age help staff to provide educational experiences that are appropriate and stimulating. This understanding makes it possible to illuminate certain aspects of present thinking about curriculum, as we discuss later. Bruner (1984, p. 181) speaks of putting the learner at the centre of a 'new curriculum' and rejects the notion of the adult's superiority in thinking. Egan (1988, p. 191) asks 'What, then, will a curriculum look like that is designed to bring childhood to ripeness within the child while at the same time moving children from an oral towards a literate and scientific culture?'

Some fundamentals of learning

There are certain understandings about young children's learning processes which from their nature demand a particular curricular response. These principles of teaching and learning might be summed up in the following way.

The social nature of the teaching/learning relationship

Young children learn in contact with other people, whether parents, teachers or peers; the quality of relationships is crucial in provision for them. The partnership with parents and the social and natural environment in which the education is to take place must emphasize the importance of the way in which these young children, who are taking their first steps in education at school, are moving into the world of education as a social venture. Provision for them must take account of the vast range of experiences that each has had before coming to school and must be provided in such a way as to put this experience at the forefront of the curriculum. There must be plentiful opportunity for spontaneous play, in which children and adults can discover what the educational experience may mean in terms of the individual child's understanding of the world. Recent research, along with other developments such as the reassessment of the work of Vygotsky (Bruner and Haste, 1987, for instance), draw attention to the socially-constructed nature of knowledge and to the way in which the level of young children's cognitive operations is determined by the meaningfulness of the context of the experience, and the social relationship between the child, other children and the adult with whom the learning is taking place. This need can only be met by a curriculum which has a model of the child as meaning-maker and the practitioner as negotiator between the child's meanings and the world as adults understand it.

My experience in teaching adults who have difficulty with reading and writing suggests that the influential nature of the relationship is not confined to the youngest learners, although their developmental degree of dependency is much greater. It is impossible to help someone with their writing without knowing their motivation to learn, what it is they wish to write, and sharing the importance they attach to it. Teaching secondary children works on the same principle; a good teaching relationship with a group of secondary children implies first establishing with them that the teacher is interested in them as individuals and in their intentions and ideas about their education.

This is even more the case with children under eight, because they are much more dependent on adults than older children are.

They depend physically, emotionally, socially, intellectually and communicatively. Young children learn and develop through contact with other people, whether parents, practitioners or other children; the quality of relationships is crucial in provision for them, and this includes the working co-operation between staff and parents. The high priority given to personal relationships by practitioners extends to the construction of a curriculum which reflects this. It also means giving a very high priority to the involvement of parents, however this is possible. This is essential if the first steps in learning outside the home are to be a success.

Learning is both a shared and an autonomous process

Young children are active and independent thinkers, who learn from communicating in real situations and handling real materials and objects, and by independent and spontaneous exploration, representation and play. Young children need a curriculum which offers them a range of first-hand experiences through freedom to explore and use a well-planned educational environment. Physical development and active exploration of the world through contact with the outside environment are fundamental; the materials and real-world technology for expressing meaning in a wide range of ways are necessary if children are to be able to be the authors of their own representations of the world. Both the curriculum and the creative environment need to be broadly-based and oriented towards the process of independent thought by which the child becomes conscious not only of the world around but also of the other minds around. This is so important a factor in developing awareness of thinking as a process in itself (through beginning to know that other minds can think and feel differently) that Dunn (1988, pp. 173–4) has suggested that this achievement should be designated as a new 'stage' in children's understanding.

Anyone who has tried to explain something to a learner of any age will know how hard it is for new material to be understood without actively 'making it one's own' in whatever way is appropriate to the learner's stage of development and interests. Everyone learns best through a focus of personal interest and in the context of their own unique experience of the world, and everyone has their own level of understanding of the world into which new ideas and information, skills and techniques, must be fitted.

The place of play in the curriculum

The developmental significance of play has already been explored in Chapter 3; at this point in our investigation of early learning it is important to get an idea of its role in the whole process of developing the curriculum.

Young children in the early years of schooling require classroom provision which places play at the centre of its educational input, not on the outskirts and for relief only, and not in a way which is so tightly controlled by adults that children cannot use it to explore what is most important to them. Play is the way young children bring their experiences and reflections upon the world into continuity with their own lives and interests. As the partner of independent enquiry, play must be recognized as the major factor in learning. The cultural bases of experience at home demand of children that they learn through play with each other about how common experience is to be found within different cultures and different languages. Of all the provision that could be made to help children become resourceful, creative and adaptable people, play provision is the most essential. All children play in order to understand and respond to experience; later success in adapting to change and responding to problems calls upon the same qualities of imaginative exploration of reality. We may recall here the high priority placed on adaptability in employees by employers.

For practitioners, play is invaluable as a teaching tool. It supports children in the transition from home to the group setting, enabling them to bring their home learning to bear on their new challenges, and to show their full range of competence. The tragedy of under-achievement should alert us all to the need to be sure that our planning is appropriate for children's levels of competence, yet repeatedly we learn that practitioners often underestimate children (Tizard and Hughes, 1984; Wells, 1987). This applies just as much to children with learning difficulties as to others. The imaginative side of play, and the way it involves and motivates children, enables practitioners to learn much from observing them. Observations of play give practitioners the information and understanding they need in order to shape their plans to children's learning needs.

The appropriate curriculum for both nursery and infant children is one which sets out to achieve the following, within a supportive social setting and in relationships that are both warm and stimulating. The curriculum should:

- foster independent enquiry and activity in the handling of real materials and objects in a context for safe questioning;
- encourage and support play in whatever way seems of interest to children because it is seen as central to their learning;
- envisage a role for the adult negotiating between what is understood about the children's level of operation and concerns and what is known about the world they are exploring;
- recognize that the child's knowledge and understanding are built up by interaction with the world in the context of personal relationships, of which the fundamental one is with the parents.

The individual, personal, spontaneous, and creative nature of this learning requires a curriculum which is not seen simply in terms of particular knowledge or skills to be acquired but in terms of the negotiation between the child and the adult of meaning about the world, about how people work and about the child's self-knowledge. Recent thinking links the nature of the curriculum with human learning processes in this way; see, for instance, Eisner (1996) and Egan (1988). In this curriculum, the individual, personal, spontaneous, and creative nature of play makes it an essential. It is the way in which children make what they are learning their own (as long as practitioners think through their play provision and their own role in it). It is also the way in which practitioners can come to a better understanding of how children's minds are working, and which are the most suitable ways to take their learning forward.

How developmental approaches underpin subject learning

Now that the National Curriculum and the Desirable Outcomes require a particular content in education in the early years, the connections between these subject-oriented approaches and the developmental approach of the early years curriculum need to be explored.

It has been explained above that all the disciplines of knowledge can be traced in children's experiences and actions from birth onwards. Developmental approaches are not, therefore, opposed to subject knowledge, but rather have the potential to make the learning of the different disciplines more effective by showing how children will find it easiest to learn. There are different versions of the developmental approach in the early years, but all have in common a characteristic set of principles to do with children's learning. These principles emphasize that young children are active and independent players and thinkers, who learn from handling real materials, objects and situations and through their own spontaneous exploration, representation and play. They assert that the curriculum needed for the education of young children is one that enables the child's predominant interests and dispositions to determine the immediate focus, within the field of action constructed by the teacher.

The Early Childhood Education Forum's *Quality in Diversity* project, circulated in draft for consultation in 1997, has drawn together the beliefs of the full range of practitioners working with children between birth and the age of eight. The participants have expressed their principles in terms of Foundations for Early Learning, and have elaborated more specific Foundation Goals from each Foundation. Most of the Foundation Goals relate to distinct areas of knowledge as well as to children's learning. Within the whole set of the Foundation Goals belonging to all five Foundations are goals relating to all the different curriculum requirements that relate to the education and care of children under eight. Most of the school subjects are represented in each Foundation.

For instance, one of the Foundations is called *Being and Becoming*: it is concerned with the belief that from birth, young children are learning self-respect, and feelings of self-worth and identity. They are learning to take care of themselves, and to keep themselves safe and well.

In this Foundation, the goals are to do with developing as an individual, and building on unique personal qualities and experiences to take part in learning with other children. The goals lay the foundations of physical achievement leading to physical education, of physical expression leading to creativity in dance, of understanding of different cultures, languages and written language leading to reading and writing, of stories and various kinds of literacy leading to English, the creative arts and information technology. Other goals are concerned with self-knowledge, with confidence in learning, with special personal interests, with learning how to avoid and reject negative stereotyping of self and of others, and with keeping safe and healthy. In other Foundations, there are goals associated with history, geography, mathematics, science and technology. (ECEF, 1997). The goals are expressed broadly, in order to take account of the great developmental range, special needs, particular experiences and inheritances in children under eight.

How children progress with the support of the goals

The goals stand within the structure of the Foundations, which places children's development and learning side by side. This, and the way that different aspects and stages of subject disciplines are present in the goals, enables practitioners to use their own judgement about what is the appropriate level of learning for children. The subjects are embedded in the Foundations, and this provides progression at the child's own pace through the various kinds of curriculum that there are for children's learning in the different age-phases and settings. The Foundations show a continuous progression. In science, for instance, there is a continuity for each child:

- achievements based on social, emotional, communicative, physical and cognitive development leading to exploration and investigation of people and objects in the world around (birth to three-year-olds);
- scientific and technological areas of learning and experience in the curriculum as described by HMI (DES, 1989c) (three- to four-year-olds);
- knowledge and understanding of the world in the Desirable Outcomes (SCAA, 1996) (four- to five-year-olds);
- Science, Technology and Information Technology in Key Stage 1 of the National Curriculum (five- to eight-year-olds).

Conclusion

The application of developmental goals such as those of *Quality in Diversity* to whatever curriculum is followed will depend on the practitioner's perceptions of children's capacities, needs and interests at their existing ages, levels of experience and stages of development. Practitioners bring together their understanding of development with their knowledge of the subjects of the curriculum. Children can be tracked in their progress along this path, with their own 'significant achievements' marked by practitioners (Hutchin, 1996).

The next chapter discusses what such a curriculum looks like in practice, and how it enables practitioners to be sure that children are achieving their best.

Further reading

Hutchin, V. (1996) *Tracking Significant Achievement: the Early Years*, Hodder and Stoughton, London.
Fisher, J. (1996) *Starting from the Child?* Open University Press, Buckingham.

For discussion

Fisher (1996) gives an example of a history task to reconstruct what took place in an accident from the available evidence, such as the contents of the dead man's wallet. She highlights the importance of the practitioner's role in reminding children of the necessity for the evidence to be reliable, in challenging their reasoning and in focusing on the particular historical understanding and skill for which she had planned the activity. She shows the links between planning in advance, extending children's learning at the time and assessing their learning after completing the activity.

What understandings about the early years curriculum is this founded on?

What understandings of history as a discipline confirm the value of this approach?

5

Making the Curriculum Work

Providing an early years curriculum

The coming of the subject-based National Curriculum has caused early years practitioners and researchers to examine more closely the roots of the disciplines of knowledge in children's early experiences. Connections between developmentally appropriate provision and subject learning are not hard to trace, but successful implementation of the curriculum is dependent on the practitioner's own activity in bringing the two together.

Maintaining a high standard of record-keeping is essential, but good records depend on other professional characteristics. The records provide the evidence on which to judge existing provision, monitor children's learning, plan for the future and evaluate our own expertise; the quality of this evidence and the perceptiveness of our interpretations of it uphold the quality of the records. More will be said later about observation; first, we will highlight what it is that is being looked for, and how to make use of what we see.

It is the quality of our knowledge of children's development and the subject disciplines which enable us to plan and provide the curriculum, to observe children's response, and to interpret what we observe.

Many publications demonstrate the way that the subject disciplines are present in children's learning from their earliest days. Trevarthen (1993) shows how communication between baby and mother is the prototype of conversational exchange (later, 'Speaking and Listening' NC, English, Key Stage 1), and he traces the foundations of musical awareness in the rhythm, pitch and intonation of mothers' and babies' voices (later, NC Music, Key Stage 1). He also shows how the spontaneous play activities of the mother with her over-two can involve mathematical ideas as well as play tutoring in social and emotional behaviour. Goldschmied (1993) shows babies exploring objects and encountering their mathematical, scientific and technological natures. She also shows (1992) older children selecting and combining objects on the basis of their physical characteristics, establishing both the nature of the materials (later NC Science, Key Stage 1) and how they themselves can manipulate, combine and sort them. Matthews (1994) shows how drawing and painting (later NC Art, Key Stage 1) express children's ideas and feelings about the world from their earliest mark-making.

The tasks of the practitioner

The challenge is, therefore, not to make children learn about the subject disciplines; they are already involved in this. The challenge is to provide for their learning with others in educational settings by drawing on their learning at home. There are four tasks in this: planning the curriculum, organizing and resourcing the learning environment, responding to and interacting with the children, and finally, evaluating and developing each of the first three tasks.

Task 1: planning the curriculum

The previous chapter has analysed in general terms the stages of the planning process, beginning with the principles upon which the curriculum is based. Now we look at the more specific aspects of providing for learning.

If it is accepted that children are already started on their learning in the subject disciplines, the planning process can be seen as maintaining and extending this learning. Before children enter the setting, home visits and consultations with parents should provide a broad profile of each child's experiences of informal learning at home (and sometimes also of formal learning with parents and other family members), and of each one's achievements, interests, special expertise and any difficulties or disabilities to be taken into consideration.

The practitioners can now plan how the setting will bring this learning, which has taken place at home up to the age of three, into the new group learning context. As explained above (p. 51), many practitioners begin with statements of principle. These often encompass aims for children's general development, and cite examples of how children learn to show how this development will be enhanced (EYCG, 1992). In many local authority documents, these statements are followed by subject-specific goals for learning, often derived from the statutory requirements for the age-phase, such as the Children Act, 1989, the Desirable Outcomes or the National Curriculum.

For a group providing for under-threes, whether it is in a child-minder's home or a nursery, crèche or playgroup, the Children Act does not specifically require that any subject be taught. Most groups rely on the categories of development established by Susan Isaacs (1929, 1930, 1933), which are the emotional, social, communicative, intellectual and physical areas of development. For a group with three- and four-year-olds, the HMI 'Areas of Learning and Experience' (DES, 1989), which used to be standard for most nurseries, playgroups and maintained nursery education, are now co-existing with or being replaced by the Desirable Outcomes for settings for four-year-olds. Reception classes in infant schools have by far the largest numbers of four-year-olds, and here the Desirable Outcomes, which are intended to prepare children for the National Curriculum, must co-exist with the downward pressure of formal schooling. No statements of principle or about appropriate methods give guidance as to how to teach the Desirable Outcomes, and practitioners have to make their own decisions. Groups providing for children between five and eight range from maintained and private infant classes to after-school and play provision. In school, Key Stage 1 of the National Curriculum is required; out of school, the Children Act, 1989 is the only requirement.

Quality in Diversity in Early Learning (ECEF, 1997 draft) is unusual in that its five statements of principle, its Foundations of Early Learning, are subsequently set out as specific goals. The five Foundations are developmental, and very broad, because they cover the full age-range from birth to eight. Each is therefore to be interpreted by practitioners according to what is appropriate for children's particular stages of development as well as the relevant statutory requirements. For instance, one Foundation reads:

> *Being active and expressing*: from birth, young children are mentally and physically active. They are learning to express their ideas, thoughts and feelings, alone and with others, in a variety of ways.

The goals which follow from it include:

- discovering and practising their mental and physical powers;
- expressing their ideas, feelings and emotional needs through a variety of forms (verbal and non-verbal, symbolic and imaginative play);

Mapping the world of fact and feeling

I have in my possession a drawing by a girl of four, given to me on a visit to a nursery. It is made up of straight lines intersecting in a kind of triangle shape, with lines leading off and converging. The girl told me that it was a 'village with three corners'. It was where she had been at the weekend with her family. A London nursery school observed the same kind of interest in mapping in their own children, and incorporated it into their planning, starting with visits of small groups of children to familiar aspects of the local environment. They would be enabling children to meet the Desirable Outcome requirements for 'Knowledge and Understanding of the World' through local visits and explorations including using information technology to represent where they had been. Some of the requirements for mathematics would be met through thinking about shapes, position, size and quantity (how many trees on the grass patch?). Language and literacy requirements would be met through talking about experiences and ideas, using books, and using pictures, symbols and words to communicate meaning. The personal and social requirements could be met through the group work and through the personal aspects of the work. Both the large-scale and the fine manipulative movements required in physical development could be provided for indoors and in the outdoor environment. Technology, which is under-represented in the Desirable Outcomes, would be provided for through modelling some of the aspects of the physical environment that were encountered.

Children would be able to choose which if any of these aspects to join in with, and would be able to contribute their own ideas and initiatives. This open-ended quality of pre-school education can make adults anxious; teachers may wonder how they can be sure they have taught all the children what they need to know, parents may fear that this informal approach is delaying their children's start on schooling. Yet, there could not be more 'real learning' than there is in the individual contributions that children make. A group of boys decided to make a map of the outdoor climbing equipment; another boy decided to record on paper a model that he had made so that he did not forget what he had done.

- representing their ideas and feelings through a variety of symbolic systems (spoken and sign languages, paint, dance, music, rhythm, imaginative play, mark-making, mathematical and other written languages).

The advantage of *Quality in Diversity in Early Learning* as an approach is that its goals challenge practitioners to plan for children to have appropriate encounters with the full range of subject disciplines within a framework that gives the highest priority to each child's own development and individual experience.

An example now follows, to show how planning from children's interests can bridge the gap between personal and group learning, and to show the range and depth of learning that can be achieved without sacrificing children's personal motivation to learn.

Task 2: resourcing and organizing the learning environment

Whether the setting is a small group with a childminder or a larger group in maintained, private or voluntary premises, the curriculum has to provide a bridge from home-based and personal learning to aims for learning shared with the group and then on to aims set by the wider community for children of compulsory school age. These 'bridges' that help children through the transitions are the developmentally appropriate activities that practitioners provide.

The early years curriculum is provided through the indoor and outdoor environment; this involves setting out a range of educational areas within and between which children are normally able to pursue their interests at will. The day's programme and the classroom organization are constructed to support this. These areas usually include the following:

- creative or craft area, often organized on a 'workshop' basis;
- book area:
- writing and drawing area;
- construction area, with large and small blocks for building;
- puzzles and games;
- role play provision;
- miniature world provision;
- malleable materials;
- outdoor play area with climbing, digging, imaginative and games equipment available throughout the day;

- natural world materials (clay, sand, water, earth, growing things) and equipment.

Through the provision of resources arranged in this or similar ways the early years practitioner builds an educational environment for the children. This environment has within it representative elements of the main aspects of the world which our culture wishes children to know about. The classroom environment corresponds to our inherited academic disciplines and bodies of knowledge in various ways. The younger the children, the more the adults will examine the provision that is made to ensure that it meets their needs, but each age-group, in its own way, needs to have access to this range of opportunities.

HMI in their publication *The Education of Children under Five* (DES, 1989c), divide the aspects of knowledge into broad areas: personal, human and social learning and experience; language and literacy; mathematical learning and experience; scientific learning and experience; technological learning and experience; and aesthetic, creative and physical learning and experience. These areas may be seen as a framework within which a suitable curriculum for young children could be developed, but, as explained earlier, the individual interests and learning needs of the children would be a balancing influence on the curriculum as it was developed.

Initially we tend to think of certain areas as being connected with certain kinds of learning. In terms of the indoor and outdoor environment the following connections might be made:

- creative or craft area, often organized on a 'workshop' basis – creative and aesthetic, technical, language and maths;
- book area, writing and drawing area – language and literacy, personal, human and social learning;
- construction area, with large and small blocks for building – technical, mathematical, language, personal, human and social;
- puzzles and games – maths, language, personal, human and social (co-operation, for instance);
- imaginative play provision – personal, human and social, maths, language;
- miniature world provision – personal, human and social, maths, language;
- malleable materials – scientific, creative, technical, maths, language;

- outdoor play area with climbing, digging, imaginative and games equipment – scientific, physical, personal, human and social, language;
- natural world materials (sand, water, earth, growing things) and equipment – scientific, maths, personal, human and social, language.

On further reflection children's responses show that all the different disciplines may connect with each of these areas of provision. In addition to this, the way that children form ideas about the world through their own mental and physical activity means that each of these areas needs to be approached from a child development perspective as well as a subject-based one. Each of the areas listed above is capable of explication in full to show how this can be done. There is not enough space to examine each in full, so the following analysis of curricular provision in the outdoor environment will serve both as an introduction to some fundamental principles of the early years curriculum and as an argument for its own development as a high-priority area.

They don't go to school just to run about, do they?

In Chapter 2 we saw how young children often express their ideas through movements; one child represented her family through a circle which enclosed a named dot to stand for each member, while another played with the idea of being inside his room's playground or outside it. Those who wish children to develop their thinking skills would do well to make sure that they have continuous access to a well thought out playground, where adults understand how to support their learning. The beginnings of mathematics and logic, and of scientific categorization, lie in children's ability to say what goes with what, and for what reason. In moving their bodies in the playground or their brushes on the paper children express the way that they are learning how to handle these ideas. In noting these activities and learning strategies adults can find out how best to support and extend this thinking. When the ideas that begin in movement are extended with adult help into games, jokes, stories and puzzles the child is enabled to translate this learning into forms in which it can be applied to other situations. The beginning of mathematical thinking is not the gathering of lots of red objects into one heap and blue ones into another, but the encircling of a space to represent the classroom

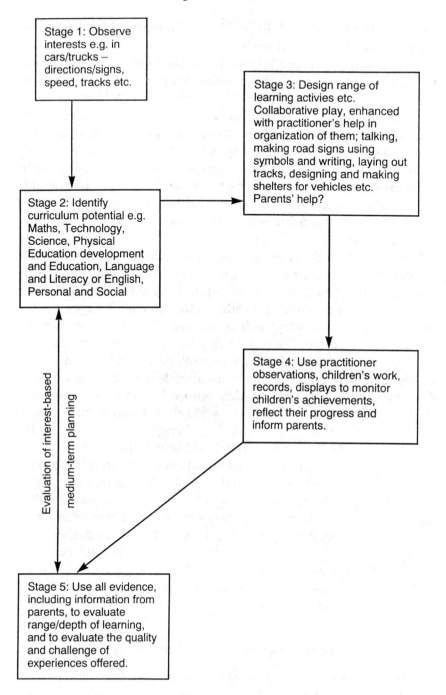

Figure 5.1 Planning in the Early Years – Children's Interests (medium-term plans)

'and this is you (the adult) and this is me and this is Jake and Harry's not here – he's at home.'

Within one group of children there are likely to be many different ways of exploring the possibilities of a well-planned playground. The opportunity for movement of all kinds will be explored if the area is sufficiently interesting – children do not 'practise' as adults do but they do develop movements if they feel the need to do so. The greatest spur is imaginative play, especially with other children. Crouching, leaping, twirling, climbing can be done for enjoyment or to achieve a goal, or they can be part of play – in the pursuit of which children will take themselves to higher levels of effort and achievement than they would for any adult-organized game.

When one says that outdoor learning environments are vital for mental development people do not always envisage the intellectual stimulus of all kinds that is implied. Now that science is seen as an important part of every child's education at all stages, knowledge of the natural world will be seen as a benefit to be obtained from the playground. But in a much wider sense the chance to play with virtually unrestrained movement gives children the even greater benefit of enriching their learning through this very powerful means. The interests of Giles, whose learning was discussed earlier (see pp. 5–7), illustrate how children's particular concerns can form the basis of a full and challenging curriculum in the outdoor and indoor learning areas as shown in Figure 5.1.

Making provision in the areas noted above has to take account, then, of the role each can play in the child's development as well as the meaning each area has in the adult world. Bringing the two together involves negotiating between them. There is no area where a more sensitive approach is needed than in that of literacy. Here, not only are there many opportunities for practitioners and children to explore and think about different aspects of reading and writing – there are also the great expectations of parents and community to relate to as well.

Task 3: responding to children – literacy

In thinking about how to provide stimulus and support for young children's growing awareness of the role of literacy in our lives we find the double nature of education becomes an important guide to action. We have both to demonstrate the value we place upon the child's own achievements, home language and culture and to lead the child on towards a deeper understanding and a greater capacity in the public modes as well. We need our knowledge of how learners learn and our knowledge of each particular learner to help us here. We also need our understanding of literacy as an active force in people's living and thinking – its enjoyableness, its practical importance, its role as a cultural influence and as the source of intellectual challenge.

We need as well to be clear about the value of recognizing children's early attempts at writing for themselves and at becoming confident 'readers' of the books that they enjoy. Being literate means much more than being able to write letters or sound them out; it means knowing how these sounds relate to written messages and what this means in terms of the child's own enjoyment and interests. All of this should be founded in the earliest days. Children need books from babyhood, as Butler (1988) shows. They need the shared ceremony and focus of a story, the regular turning of the pages; they need the closeness; they need the colours and liveliness of the illustrations; they need the rich interest of the characters in the pictures; they need the order and rhythm of the story; they need the rhythm and sound of the text, with its expected exclamations and different voices; they need the characters and events to be applied to their own lives; they need the story as a reference point between themselves and their closest people. As they get older, this intimate interaction extends step by step, but should never lose its quality of personal involvement. When children know what reading and writing offer them, they will have reason to learn how letters are formed and used; then, the help of a practitioner will be sought, perhaps at first to write down in public mode what a child has written in beginning or 'emergent' writing. Whenever appropriate to the young child's needs help can be given with the encoding and decoding skills that are so useful to children in giving them access to written material of all kinds. Some want to write specific things; Aaron, aged three, could write his name, and asked to be shown how to write 'Mummy'. He could then name his pictures and mark the one for his mother. Weeks later he asked how 'from' was written, in order to write on a special picture for her – 'Mummy from Aaron'. Other children approach through stories, learning them by heart from repetition, and later associating the story-line with particular words. They can often then make comparisons between the look of a known word and a new one, as they can with similar children's names such as Charles and Charlotte.

A practitioner who aims at both the child development and the public mode aspects of literacy will start with the natural way in which reading and writing occur in daily life. The children will need to see how these processes fit into their lives so that they can know how to use them. The enjoyment and warmth of a shared story, or of the retelling of something that happened yesterday, and the excitement of seeing how written messages can make things happen – these are the bases of literacy.

This early work is the start of reading and writing in the most profound sense. In spite of the way that until quite recently it was thought that formal reading and writing were the only kind of literacy possible for young children, early years practitioners and infant teachers have begun to see children's original and spontaneous attempts at literacy-related marks as great strides in understanding. The children who make marks on paper to which they attribute linguistic significance have already cracked the puzzle; they know that the marks on paper in books, newspapers, shopping lists and on hoardings have meaning. With children at this stage, adults indeed are often asked to decode marks which do not have the kind of meaning that children have learned to expect – car registration plates, for instance. We adults also get caught out in this way ourselves, when we peer at minute letters on a piece of official paper only to find that they are a reference sequence.

As Whitehead (1990) says, the significance of this has not been lost on professionals interested in the development of literacy in infant and junior schools.

> The recent emphasis on young children's potential interest in literacy and their experiments with significant marks and the possibilities of writing has aroused new interest in what goes on in nursery schools and classes. In terms of teaching literacy, the centre of gravity has suddenly shifted to the 'early' early years and nursery teachers and nurses have to consider the issues that face all teachers of beginning writers. These issues can no longer be left for infant and first-school teachers to concentrate on.
>
> (p. 191)

Elsewhere, the discussion of Tony's interest in labelling files is seen as an example of the need to develop a curriculum that relates to children's activity in their learning (see p. 136–8). The role of the practitioner's planning in developing the curriculum has, in the same way, to take account of everything that embodies a literacy experience in children's lives. This means that the home and the local community can be seen as a rich resource to draw on. Although parents and professionals may not always agree as to the best way to teach reading and writing, they can agree on the importance of their children's learning. In fact, as I suggest in Chapter 7, each may have good reasons for what is done in the two different domains. The vital link between the language and culture of the home and that of the setting is what must be preserved. For children who are bilingual, the mother tongue must be acknowledged, even if, like some, the child prefers to use English. For children whose culture may have different strengths from the majority one – a powerful oral tradition like Sonny Boy's, for instance (Cousins, 1990), or unusual and compelling folk tales such as the Anansi tales from West Africa and the Caribbean – these aspects must form part of the practitioner's expectation of literacy. If not, the practitioner runs counter to the strengths of the home culture, and this is a battle that none of us either can or ought to win.

This outline poses another level of thought to contrast with the analysis based on subject disciplines outlined above (p. xvi–xvii). The complexity of the curriculum can be seen in this. Both contribute to successful provision, and practitioners have to be committed to each equally. Literacy is not just having a book corner and sitting children down to write; it is to do with understanding what literacy is about and what it can do for us. In the list above (p. 68–9), only one area is specifically concerned with literacy, but in fact they all are or could be. If written symbols can convey words spoken and experiences gained to other people at other times in other places, then they can be involved in a description of how a model was made, a recipe for a cake, the details of the construction and purpose of a block building, the story of an outing with parents, a tribute to children who have left, the labels on the stored materials and resources – the list can be extended. The most important feature of all, which unites all provision, is the contribution literacy makes to what might be called 'The story of Me'. Children sometimes say, 'Mrs. Smith, Mrs. Smith, you know me?' 'Yes, Lisa, I know you all right.' 'Well, I went to the circus yesterday . . .'. The challenging business of becoming a known person in a big social group can be made more easy for children if their identities can be communicated through material about themselves. Lisa's trip to the circus could be one such subject. In this way, literacy will be part of Lisa's good experiences, and will be more likely to remain so.

Task 4: evaluating and adapting

Where children are expected to be active learners, the knowledge which they are expected to be learning is presented in the environment in which they are active. The teacher, by constructing a well-planned classroom and outdoor environment, offers a view of the range of learning appropriate for children of this age. The well-constructed early years environment, the embodiment of the curriculum, should be like a model of the world as we can best understand it.

Within this environment the nursery practitioner works to develop the curriculum through evaluation based on observation of children's activity and interests; this makes it possible to assess their levels of understanding and what are the most likely avenues of learning for them. This process of initial planning, observation and response is the heart of the dynamic process of the nursery and early years curriculum. How this works in practice may be seen from the following example.

Evaluating and developing a curriculum for young children

During October work was undertaken with groups of the children who were interested to clear a small plot of ground which had been neglected. Weeds and self-seeded plants were removed and the ground dug. A small compost heap was created with the resulting grass, leaves and so on; the children found it very hard to believe that such materials would turn into 'new earth for the plants' but they were able to keep an eye on the heap throughout the winter and to report when any item of greenery had 'gone'. Digging over the plot showed that there were many bulbs there; these were sorted for size and replanted so that the smaller ones were at the front of the bed. A little path was built from bricks laid flat so that the children could follow a trail in and out of the remaining plants, some of which were tall enough to give children a feeling of going into a hidden place away from others in the playground. The bulbs had not been the only underground treasure discovered; many 'minibeasts' were found, and temporary homes constructed in the classroom before they were returned to the earth.

In order to support and extend the interest so far generated a digging patch was organized and tools obtained, with suitable containers and procedures for looking after finds. It seemed as if this was going to be the only way the garden plot developed until providentially there was a visit from a police horse, which obligingly left a heap of dung. When making the compost heap the children had been told that there were other things beside compost that were good for soil, and they had expressed disbelief that anyone could put dung onto their garden on purpose. This was now done, amidst general amazement, and during the following winter months of rain and frost children kept reporting on what was happening to the dung; they found it hard to believe that it would go into the earth.

Chantelle, 4 years 6 months, was particularly horrified by the dung and particularly interested in what happened to it. She frequently reported on its progress and would drag members of staff over to see what was going on. After the spring half term she went straight to the spot, returning to announce 'The poo's gone!' She took a trowel and dug around the spot, finding no trace of the dung. However, she did find worms, which she carried around in her hand. Making provision for her to install them in the classroom and to look after them became a focus of interest for other children as well. It was very hard for her to accept that they needed conditions other than her warm and enthusiastic hand if they were to survive, and this provided for Chantelle, and for other children, another experience of the otherness of other life-forms. Woodlice were the next recruits, on a temporary basis, and later the first ants. This proved a very useful theme with children who did not always engage with staff in their activities, and small boxes of ants became an opportunity to relate more closely. In the summer it was found that the compost heap had matured to a sufficient degree to provide soil to fill the insides of tyres as containers for plants in the playground, and children helped to do this.

The ongoing evaluations based on observations of the children enabled the curriculum to be progressively adapted in plans, resources and organization and in responses to children's initiatives. Interest in the compost heap and the dung led to a greater emphasis on soil than had been anticipated. Finding small creatures in the earth gave the indoor focus a push towards natural history and the need to care thoughtfully for other forms of life, and it also led to a focus on digging outdoors – digging for exploration rather than as part of gardening. The process of evaluation will be further described in Chapter 8.

Conclusion

Practitioners work to provide the physical environment and the setting, the materials and the cognitive context for all this intellectual activity; they structure the children's understanding of the world by structuring their environment. The effort and thought they put into enriching the outdoor area with provision for scientific investigation, for instance, embodies for children what the scientific approach to the world is all about. Again, teachers also take a role in the child's exploration of the environment, calling attention for example to aspects of the natural world by saying 'Let's find out, shall we? How do you think we could find out what this beetle likes to eat?' A whole encapsulation of the idea of objective investigation of the world is in that simple-seeming interaction. And how often the simple-seeming interactions of early childhood turn out to be statements about the world and our place in it when you examine them. We must, I believe, plan for these interactions as carefully as we plan for the environment; we need for instance to be free, or plan with others that we should be free, to fulfil this vital role, often participating in the play or helping in the exploration. We act as resource-banks, models, guides, supporters and researchers, but most of all as informed enablers and instigators in the children's learning.

Further reading

Whitebread, D. (1996) Young Children Learning and Early Years Teaching in D. Whitebread (ed.) *Teaching and Learning in the Early Years*, Routledge, London.

For discussion

Whitebread (1996) emphasizes in his Introduction, 'Young Children Learning and Early Years Teaching', the importance of children feeling in control of their learning. He associates this with empowering them as learners. Yet so often the burden of over-prescribed curriculum content leads us to assume the inadequacy of children's existing knowledge and competence.

At one nursery school, a display of different minerals was set up within easy reach of the children. In addition to the minerals which had been borrowed from a museum, there were magnifiers, measuring and weighing equipment, reference books open and within reach and drawing and writing materials. The display was added to by the children as they found stones and other natural and made objects in the earth at home and in the playground.

In the past, practitioners have assumed the link between children's active early learning and their later formal achievements because, to them, it was obvious. Nowadays, we have to be more precise. How could the children's own contributions be the starting-point of a planned curriculum which would empower them *and* enable parents and practitioners to feel confident in their academic progress?

6

Observation and Assessment

Observation is the foundation of education in the early years, in that it is through recording and reflecting on children's activities and interests that we can gather the information necessary for the construction of an appropriate curriculum for them. It is also the way in which we can gather the material from which to make informed professional judgements about children's progress, and about how to help them best. Observation, assessment and the development of an appropriate curriculum all fit together. This is how those who teach children under the age of eight provide an educational experience which stimulates and challenges them. The crucial issues of how educational quality is ensured and of how children's exceptional gifts and needs are provided for are resolved in this way in the education of the under-fives.

This may be seen as a controversial statement; it appears to run counter to the belief that adults ought to decide in advance precisely what children should learn and check subsequently whether they are in fact doing so. It also challenges the received wisdom that young children do only a simple kind of learning, since – as the examples to follow will show – the kind of learning that is involved is clearly both deep and broad.

Observation is thus linked with a particular view of assessment, and with a particular model of the curriculum. Both in relation to the curriculum in general and to our present topic of assessment, the National Curriculum offers us models in which there are many issues to be discussed and questioned. This chapter will look at some current ideas about assessment in general in order to examine the strength of the position outlined above.

Controversial issues concerning assessment

The field of assessment today presents us with some sharply differing views. It is hard to choose among them without some way of judging how useful each is likely to be. We need to ask the question 'What is the purpose of this assessment?' before we make any decisions. Moreover, there are curriculum models implied in the many decisions that have to be taken about assessment (see Fisher, 1996, pp. 151–8, for a detailed analysis).

Education is a complex and sophisticated business. It is not just about telling the learners what we think they ought to know, but about finding out what learning is already going on and linking this with new learning. All learners, whether young children or adults, come to their teachers with ideas about the world which they have developed through their own experiences and interests, and it is on these existing ideas that the new learning must be built. When people have difficulty in understanding something new, their teachers go back to what they understand well in order to extend the understanding to the new material.

The work of the early years practitioner

Children under eight bring with them a great deal of learning already established, and developmental methods of teaching aim to build on this learning. In order to know how to build on this foundation practitioners have to find out about children's interests and ideas, abilities and experiences, families and friendships. This involves the practitioner in observing how children behave in the setting and the playground, on the way in and as they go home. What parents have to share with practitioners is of great importance – the home and local community are where children spend the majority of their time, and the influence of parents and the community is in many ways greater than that of the practitioner and the setting.

Children tell us about themselves through their behaviour, and there are clues to how we can best teach them to be found in their play and social interactions, in their conversations and the stories they bring from home, in the way they use opportunities to explore new areas of learning and in the way they create stories, pictures, models and music, and recreate those that are already familiar.

Making educational decisions

Effective education is not about the simple transmission of knowledge but about the exercise of professional expertise and insight in order to follow up and extend the learner's existing knowledge and understanding. Building on the foundations of each child's learning means that we have to be able to say what each has achieved and what it would be appropriate to lead on to next.

Teaching, if it is to be effective, must be targeted at the learner's educational needs and stage of understanding. In order to target teaching appropriately we have to use a range of methods of assessing children's progress, relevant experiences and interests, all of which will give helpful information about how to extend their learning.

Those who teach need to discover what the learner already knows and can do. As Fisher (1996) points out, this is not something that happens just once in a child's education; every time a practitioner begins to teach a new area of knowledge, the first question must be 'What do you know about this already?' The question is broader and even more important when both the topic and the practitioner are new to the children. 'What kind of a learner are you, and what learning experiences have you had?' are questions which need to be answered before decisions can be made about how best to teach. The next question must be 'What have you achieved already? What can we build on?'

These questions point to the essential role of formative assessment in effective education. They also show the most fundamental difference between this and any other system of assessment, because they look for what the learner can, rather than cannot, do. Where careful itemization of precise targets for learning has been done, the intention is to focus upon those that the learner has not achieved. This pessimistic view reflects a fear that the learner will fall ever more behind unless there is constant pressure; my basic objection is that this is inequitable and unrealistic as an approach for under-eights. It does not reflect the way that they learn; it penalizes those whose experiences and gifts are different from those of the dominant group; it enforces a narrow performance-based interpretation of achievement which devalues the creativity, courage, self-questioning and deeply reflective feeling and thinking of young children.

The formative early years approach, however, can record the achievements of the learner in a way that reflects the pattern of each child's progress, whatever the starting point and whatever the rate of progress. This kind of assessment will guide staff to the next stage – the provision of a curriculum which can take the learner's achievements further through opportunities for new learning.

The expertise involved in assessment lies in the way in which the information gathered through observation and record-keeping is related to the child's previous achievements and development. This is how progress is monitored, and the knowledge gained about the child's progress is used to develop a curriculum that will take the child's learning further. This raises questions about how the individual child's stage of development and understanding can be provided for while other children's needs are also being met. These will be discussed in relation to curriculum development (see p. 91–7 for a fuller discussion).

It is vital to have accurate information on the children's needs. The adult plans for the arrangement of the learning environment and for the work of individual members of staff on the basis of this information. The plans are developed further using insight about the knowledge children need to acquire and in the light of this information about the individual children.

A good example of how this happens is through observation of children's play activities. The way in which children structure their own learning in play provides adults with the opportunity to learn what they are now confident about, or interested in. This understanding can be used to provide practitioners with the most meaningful context of all for extending children's thinking (see pp. 58–9).

The subject of curriculum planning is dealt with fully in Chapter 4, but it is necessary to point out here how much it depends on the quality of information about the children. The quality of the education provided lies in planning a curriculum, on a termly, weekly and daily basis, in such a way as to focus on the real meaning of experiences to each individual child. This enables practitioners to develop a curriculum from their understanding of individual children's needs and interests. Without accurate information on children's development the curriculum may quickly become dominated by adult ideas, and drift away from a focus on what children understand and can make use of. With this information it is possible to construct and subsequently develop a learning environment in which individual children can pursue their own purposes in play, exploration and other ways. This means that children's spontaneity and autonomy are fostered at the same time as their educational needs are being met.

Assessment in a wider educational context

But does this approach find any support elswhere? In 1987 the Report of the Task Group on Assessment and Testing (TGAT) outlined three essential functions of assessment for the National Curriculum: it should be formative, having a view to the learner's future development; it should be diagnostic, aiming at identification of weaknesses; it should be summative, giving assurance that the learner has reached acceptable levels of achievement. Since then, unfortunately, political emphasis on the performance of schools and other settings in 'league tables' has given value to the summative kind of assessment only. Yet practitioners persist in their efforts to suit the education to the child, and they find the formative and diagnostic aspects of assessment to be the tools that they require. They are also a part of the practitioner's tools for evaluation of their work; this will be discussed in Chapter 8.

In judging the value of any particular system of assessment these principles should be borne in mind, particularly if it is proposed that the system should have a developmental as well as a summative aspect; without a diagnostic and formative element assessment will be unable to contribute to the development of appropriate planning for children's development as individuals.

Assessment from observation

The current trend in assessment for the National Curriculum places great importance on pupils' capacity to meet certain specified criteria. If these are not achieved there is seen to be a problem. There is a place for this summative kind of assessment. Suitable subjects for this might be areas where the child's thought processes or interests needed to be broadly assessed – 'has she got some idea of fullness?' or where it would be helpful to know how much a child was participating in the range of opportunities available – 'does she leave her best-known adult to play with other toddlers?' A check-list might be constructed for children's use of outdoor playspace, or to find out whether an individual was able to find ways to build three dimensionally. Diagnostic and formative assessment, on the other hand, would be needed to find out what were the reasons for children's behaviour and to work out how adults could best provide for further learning and development. For these purposes, observation is essential.

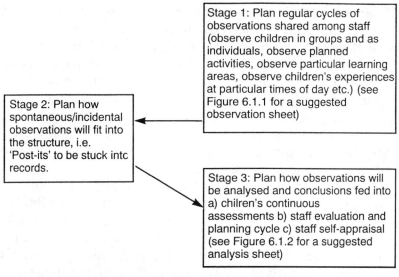

Figure 6.1.1 Planned Observation Sheet

Purpose of observation	(e.g. Ongoing assessment)
Method of observation	(e.g. 10 mins 'Target child')
Date Time	Place Programme (e.g. Storytime)
Child/children observed	
Adult/s present	Other information (e.g. From parents)
	Other observations

Figure 6.1.2 Analysis Sheet

Focus of enquiry (e.g. Outdoor play)		
Evidence presented by	Others present	
Other evidence considered (e.g. From parents or colleagues)		
Points discussed		
Action to be taken 1	by whom	when
Action to be taken 2	by whom	when
Action to be taken 3	by whom	when

Figure 6.1   Observing, Reflecting, Learning

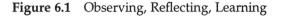

Observation-based assessment works by giving adults an insight into what the child can already do, and some clues as to what mental strategies and models are being developed. Pre-set targets rely on generalized descriptions of behaviour and avoid entering into explorations of the place of the behaviour in the child's development. From them we get a list of activities or functions, or skills or 'competences', that are or are not discernible in the child. They tell us nothing without the context – why the child undertook them or how the child seems to be choosing what to do or not to do – and could only give us a list to check off.

However, if we use very broad criteria, which ask open questions, we may be able to rely on the strengths of both methods. A list can be prepared in advance if it asks such questions as 'What activities does this child show most interest in?' and 'What play themes does this child enjoy?' or 'How does this child use representational materials like paint and clay?' Answers to these questions, reinforced with observations and examples of children's work, would help adults to understand the way the learning process was developing for that individual child. The questions could be developed as a staff activity so that each member had a say in them. In this way, practitioners would perhaps feel they had a structure to support them which would not be too rigid to adapt to each child.

Given that a high priority is placed on meeting individual emotional, social, cognitive and physical needs in the education of young children, assessment based on observation should play much the greater part, and have much more influence on judgements about children.

Education and observation

Early years expertise lies in finding out many kinds of essential information through observing children during normal educational activities. This shows children's present levels of understanding, and indicates the new areas of learning they are becoming ready for, as well as challenging teachers' expectations of individual children. With these landmarks of children's development marked out, we can begin to develop a coherent educational response to them.

How do practitioners make decisions about the educational experiences they offer their pupils? All teachers have to decide what is the most suitable way to teach their pupils, whatever age and stage they may have reached. We need to examine the idea that practitioners find out how to teach by observing their pupils; if this is the case, then observation of pupils is the most important process that teachers undertake.

Also, teachers have to be good learners from their observations in order to find out how to educate their pupils most effectively. The only way to gather evidence about how children are progressing is to observe their behaviour in different settings – in groups, as individuals, at play, in conversation, in structured teaching situations, with adults, and so on. Evidence is also collected in the form of stories, paintings, drawings, models and so on – these can be photographed, photocopied, traced or sketched by the adult if they are fragile or if the child wants to keep them.

Participant observation

Observation is a normal part of education in the early years and is essentially a process which is carried out as an integral part of teaching. This normal, everyday kind of observation consists of the adult's continuous awareness, carefully recorded each day, of what children are doing in the setting. This demands sensitivity and alertness to what is going on around, and is a vital part of professional expertise. It is dependent for its success on precise and regular record-keeping since no-one can keep all the valuable information about children's activities and interests in their head for any lengh of time. However records are kept, they need to be kept up to date regularly if they are to be any use. They must also be the basis of educational decision-making.

Ongoing daily observation is often described as 'participant observation' to make clear that it does not mean the adult withdrawing from interaction with the class. Relevant items of information are noted in the course of everyday work and jotted down at the first opportunity. These notes form the basis for assessment and planning for individuals and groups, and are carefully written into group or class plans and individual assessments.

Practitioners have an extremely busy day. How can they find time to do this, when so much of their work consists of talking to children? Observation can be built into the day if the organization is there to support it. The organization of the learning environment can contribute to giving members of staff the freedom to watch a little more, if the children are enabled to look after themselves as far as possible. Planning should encourage children to use the prepared activities independently, to fetch the additional equipment or materials they require, to think about how to tackle problems and to help each other. Naturally, they will need to be able to move freely without restrictions. The way the adults are used is also very important. The day can be planned with short times for observation by different members of staff as long as each person knows what is asked of them.

What should be noted?

Those who are responsible for the care and education of young children need to know a wide range of things about them. Social, physical and emotional development is as relevant to educational progress as is the child's growing knowledge and understanding of academic processes, and evidence both of cognitive levels and of behaviour will need to be noted. Ongoing notes can be made of whatever is relevant to the children's development; practitioners will find it helpful to make rough notes of anything they find interesting during the day, and then to write up their notes after they leave school – the sooner the better, before other experiences make the memory fade.

How can we arrive at asking particular questions about children, and how do we choose what items of behaviour to note down? There has to be a coherent approach to observation, and to assessment through observation. The coherence comes from the fact that the early years curriculum underlies both, and that they are not separate from curricular planning. As the provision is planned, with the educational content securely rooted in the activities and equipment available to the children, the criteria for assessment of the children are already built in. From the list of potential educational outcomes below can be drawn the framework for assessment that will apply to the group in general and within which staff mark and record the progress of individuals.

Developing observation and assessment from one resource area

Both wet and dry sand were available in an early years setting; some of the equipment is listed here, with the sorts of educational outcomes that were tentatively expected. It was hoped that if the materials were sufficiently exciting, they would stimulate children's imagination, provoke them to talk and challenge them to find new ways to express what they were experiencing and thinking.

Resources were accumulated and stored by the sand so that children could use them and return them without having to ask for staff help. Small amounts of each kind of resource were put out so that children had a wide choice without being overwhelmed by the amount available. Extra resources were stored out of the way in case they were needed for some special interest. Particular resources to be used in accordance with staff plans could also be put out when new ideas demanded it.

Range of resources

- Water, sticks, stones, shells, etc. These often support scientific, mathematical, technological and creative explorations of natural materials; they can also be used for sociodramatic and imaginative play.
- Large and small equipment for measuring, weighing, etc. These support scientific and mathematical investigations, and sociodramatic play.
- Containers of various sizes and shapes, rakes, moulds, etc. These are useful for mathematical, scientific, technological and creative investigations and for sociodramatic and imaginative play.
- Pouring and filling equipment. This can lead to scientific, mathematical and technological investigations and to sociodramatic and imaginative play.
- Sociodramatic play equipment (teasets, for instance). This often supports domestic, imaginative and role play, in which many mathematical and scientific insights develop as well.
- Provision for miniature world play (small figures etc). These support imaginative play, role play, imaginative representation of the world. The mathematical and linguistic experiences here are potentially very rich.

Finding out how children use resources

It must be accepted that expected outcomes do not always occur, and that the advance planning will need to be adjusted and developed in the light of children's actual responses. Play can happen in the context of almost any provision and is a particularly rewarding outcome if staff focus on what can be learned from it. Learning does not take place in separate subject compartments, of course, and staff will find that satisfactory educational experiences are

Two girls were observed using the wet sand. They began by using some small figures of workmen in hard hats with shovels. They moved sand around, then fetched some small lorries and diggers and roared these up and down the hills of sand they had created. The sand was very wet, and muddy-looking water sloshed around in pools. Suddenly, the tone of their play changed from being busy and chatty – 'My man's fallen over!' 'Quick, I'll bring my lorry to help him . . . where is he?' – to one that was more deeply involved and excited. A story began to emerge, accompanied by vigorous actions. The water apparently had to be contained at one end of the sand tray. They removed all the small figures and lorries, and set to with their hands to try to get the water into one place and contain it with sand barriers. As there was so much water, it was a constant battle, but they were not frustrated. Every time the water ran out through their dams they became more excited, and pushed it back faster. Their language was full of urgency; 'Oh no! It's pouring out again . . . build it up over here, the wall's falling down.' 'Hurry up, it's breaking through!' 'I can't hold it back, it's getting bigger and bigger.' Their movements became more and more urgent, and even-tually another member of staff had to remind them about not splashing the people nearby or getting the floor wet. This was timely, since they were so absorbed and thrilled with the drama they were enacting that they were quite unaware that sandy water was flying all over the observer and the other children near them.

The drama that they were imagining was to do with trying to control water, and with the fascinating way that it is so difficult to control. They were learning much about its properties as a natural material, and about the properties of sand, and about how the two behave together. They were finding out through physical actions what movements would help to shift the water quickly or make the sand walls firmer. Their language was expressive and dramatic, their gestures conveyed excitement. Their shared enjoyment formed a strong bond between them, and even survived the need to do some mopping-up together afterwards.

ones which engage children's imagination and encourage them to participate at their own levels and stages of development. As staff observe, they will see many different kinds of understanding and skill being developed. In particular, the more exciting and thought-provoking an activity, the more it will challenge children to develop the language in which to express what they experience. The provision itemized here is often most successful used in an imaginative or conceptual setting which will engage interest and stimulate imagination – natural materials like shells and stones in a 'seaside' setting, for instance, or linked with an exciting narrative like a dragon story (see p. 90).

For the practitioner, it was a chance to take her plans further along the lines already laid out, in a way which would be enriched by these children's vivid imagination. The sand, wet and dry, was provided continuously because of its richness as a resource for scientific and mathematical learning. The girls had experienced an exciting way to motivate children to think and learn about natural materials and their behaviour. The range of natural materials could be extended with wooden blocks, chips and sawdust; the children could bring in stones to build more walls. Work could be extended to the outdoor learning environment. But more than that, the practitioner had a story to motivate children to make these experiments. Working with the girls, she could help them to give details and characters to their story, and to draw pictures to go with it. They could, with her help, make a book, and read it to the other children. Other books and stories about containing water could be found and used. Other children's contributions to the meaning and excitement could also be recorded.

Observation and the quality of education

The quality of education is determined by the extent to which it is adapted to the learner. Each child's individual existing achievements must be recognized, and the strategies for further learning that have been established will be the ones to consider when planning for future educational provision. No amount of scholarly depth in the teacher can compensate for a shortfall in the appropriateness of the educational provision for the learner's own strengths. I say strengths, and not weaknesses, for fear of the danger of concentration on the weaknesses of learners which can easily creep in. It is not by their weaknesses that learners overcome their difficulties, but by their strengths. Although all good practitioners try to be fully aware of the limits of their learners' achievements and understandings, they have to look to what the learner *can* do for the further development in which it may be possible to overcome the existing limits.

This approach requires rigorous exploration of the learner's understandings and learning strategies, as well as an extensive experience of the general learning and development patterns of the particular age-group being dealt with.

First step – fact-finding

An example is given (expanded for comprehensibility) of how one person approached this task.

Wednesday a.m. Yesterday Sarah (4 years 4 months) and Tasneem (4 years 3 months) were pouring water through sieves and tubes at the water tray, talking about how fast the water filled up the containers underneath; they were imagining a situation in which they had to fill them up fast because 'the children' wanted a swimming pool to play in. Today the teacher has put small figures into the dry sand, along with similar pouring equipment and containers; it is hoped that the children will be stimulated by having another kind of pouring material. They are indeed attracted to the sand, along with Darren (3 years 11 months), but they note other qualities in its pouring by comparison with water – when they fill a container the sand heaps up above the edge until they smooth it down. They experiment with filling containers 'right to the top', and decanting from one into another. The theme is now 'We're the workmen, got to make it, make it all full up'. The staff note their absorption in how much is needed to fill containers of different sizes and suggest they may like to try very small teacups and bowls from the home corner as well as the containers already there. The children have an imaginative play activity with the small figures, making them cups of tea and baking them cakes; they talk about how many measures of each ingredient they need for the cake and count them as they add them.

By the end of the morning the following is noted;

General observation
Sarah and Tasneem are both confident users of the concepts of full, empty, not so much, a bit more, bigger, much bigger, smaller, much smaller, and the appropriate vocabulary. They are thinking

about volume and capacity, and about numbers in connection with this (see below for details). Their ideas about what workmen do centre on mixing activities (How is cement made?) and on getting the containers full to the top. Darren is learning alongside the girls at his own level; in the play he is getting experience of some real meaning of these terms which he will be able to use again with them and perhaps eventually by himself in the same and in other contexts. His understanding of the play scenario is not certain. Socially he has taken a step forward, and his evident enjoyment in participation in the group experience is a positive achievement.

Specific focus observed

In addition to the language used and the maths content of their experience, the children have been observing differences in the behaviour of various natural materials – the teacher plans to explore wet sand with them next as part of their growing awareness of scientific ways of looking at the world. The teacher is also very pleased with the imaginative play aspect of the use of the sand; it has been very vivid play with a lot of excitement and has also motivated the children to new learning in various ways, such as the concern to get the cake measurements right. In addition, several other children have been attracted by the interest of the tea and cooking activity and have been drawn in to discussions of a mathematical and scientific nature without being aware of it.

Forward planning

The teacher plans to build on the miniature world play with the wet sand; initially lorries and trucks, with small digging implements and figures will be provided, though the teacher feels that the play may take off in other directions later and is prepared to make other resources available. It is likely that Darren will enjoy the opportunity to continue the dry sand play so this will be resourced in the same way tomorrow; others may well join in, and if they get involved in the idea of providing for a family of small people the teacher plans to suggest they use clay or dough to make more food etc. The benefits in terms of language and co-operative activity will be great, as well as the maths and science opportunities.

The next stage – establishing what we know

The practitioner will record the learning observed for each individual, and the interests and achievements noted during the day.

Darren is a child whose progress is being very closely monitored, as he does not seem to take much part in most of the setting's activities, preferring to drift around the room or playground or stand on the edges of groups just watching. The practitioner is very pleased indeed that he has shared the play at the sand, and will note this as a definite sign of progress to relate at future discussions with other professionals.

Information on an individual child – Sarah
Sarah is socially competent in the way she negotiates what they will do next – less directive than previously. She is able to tolerate a bit of frustration in order to keep the play going – she can allow Tasneem to direct, for instance, when to hold off the water and stir more. Although he wasn't part of their play exchanges and she has been a bit exclusive in the past she doesn't mind Darren being there at all. In fact she seems to like having him around and helped him by saying 'You're our mate, aren't you?' He was thrilled.

- Play – interested in mixing activity, and in workmen as being busy and important. No details of what they were making.
- Maths and science concepts noted – full, too much, half full, bigger container takes more, lots of spoonfuls, one (or two or three) more spoonful, dry sand won't heap up in a bucket, mixing in water makes it sticky and hard to stir.
- Language – richest in play and in descriptions of how the sand feels to touch or stir (all sticky, squidgy, etc. then playing with sound of words – sticky-licky-bicky).

Other sources of information
Existing methods of assessment can draw on a wide range of information to supplement this one observation. Continuous record-keeping, however, is essential to this process.

1. Involvement of parents and of child – Sarah can chat about what they did to the sand, her mother might contribute information about her mud pies at home, or about the workmen next door.
2. Profiles involving collaboration between child, parent and teacher – the gradual exchange of information on a variety of aspects will build up an outline of the sorts of interest and achievement noted.
3. Portfolios, projects and written reports of work, often resulting from joint work by child and parent, teacher and/or other

relevant adult – an interest such as Sarah's can often be developed through making a collection of relevant objects (workman's trowel, builder's cement, etc.) and/or making a book of drawings, photos and so on.

4. Assessments from observation at different times may be either open-ended as above or directed towards a specific target – for instance, Sarah's growing social capacity with younger children might be observed.

5. Background investigations may be independent or collaborative, i.e. in work with parents and other involved professionals – if there was any reason to be concerned about progress a child could have a multidisciplinary profile built up. This will shortly take place for Darren.

Examination and testing – written and practical
Presenting children with 'show' questions is notoriously unsatisfactory since they find it hard to understand the point of such behaviour. An excellent critique of this method is implicit in the response of the reception child called Sonny Boy who asked his teacher why such daft questions were being asked. 'Why do you keep asking the kids questions when you knows all the answers? Like . . . like . . . what colour is it then? You can see for yourself its red . . . so why do you keep asking them?' (Cousins, 1990, p. 30) The questions do seem pointless if the answers are already known, and they give children difficulty since they cannot see why to answer them. There is another problem in that the questions themselves are often at a much lower level of development than what can be observed when children are free to structure their own behaviour.

Times of assessment
Making judgements in the process of assessment is something that needs to go on all the time if the education provided is to respond to children's achievements and needs; the search for guidance as to how to provide for children demands constant up-to-date information. The assessment of a child on leaving the setting is but one part of this process.

Further action that may be required – other kinds of observation
There may be times when we will want to make a more specific focus on certain aspects of children's behaviour or on classroom

developments; in this case observations can be structured in different ways. Observations may be made of a specific child, or at specific times, or in specific areas of the classroom, or at particular stages of the day. In this kind of observation, a child's behaviour may be noted every half hour, or for a full ten minutes every two hours, or the use by pupils of a certain area of the classroom may be recorded, for instance. These structured observations are in addition to the normal participant observations and will be undertaken when there is a particular reason.

The final stage – planning what to do in the future

This is the stage where knowledge about the children and about their classroom experiences meets ideas about what it is good for children to learn. Here the practitioner needs to use the insights gained from the individual children to decide how best to present new learning to them, linking it with what already makes sense to them.

How this information can be used

For the class as a whole, the staff see opportunities to extend explorations of the natural world in the classroom and in the playground through digging and construction activities, and to build in mathematical thinking through involvement in play and in functional activities such as real cooking. The creation of stories about miniature families, with miniature world play, class-made books and tapes, children's pictures and models, will offer rich opportunities for children to extend and enrich their language, use their imagination and explore various ways of representing the world in narratives, written stories, pictures, miniature versions and models.

Conclusion

The results of observation provide detailed evidence for continuous assessment. The analysis examined above has here been linked with assessment in terms of early years practice; the information gathered can also be looked at in relation to the National Curriculum attainment targets, but there is little point in this other than to reassure adults that the children are being given a well-balanced education. As may be seen from the detailed examination of work with young children in *Early Childhood Education: the Early Years Curriculum and the National Curriculum* (EYCG, 1989) it is usual to find that the requirements have been surpassed and much more achieved as well.

Working from observation-based assessment enables us to make more reliable judgement about children, and reassures us that we are doing our best to work against the undermining or twisting of our judgements by unhelpful stereotypes of children. We can also base our evaluations of our own practice on our observations, thus helping to free ourselves from domination by our own un-challenged assumptions and others' imposition of inappropriate targets for children's behaviour. These are the issues which should inform our judgement as we review the potential role of obser-vation and the assessment and evaluation possibilities that it opens to us.

The early years curriculum arises naturally from careful obser-vation, and we can best meet our responsibilities in this way. The responsibility of providing a full and rich curriculum requires us to consider how to provide a stimulating and well-founded pro-gramme; observation shows us how to link this programme with children's existing understandings so that they can make the best use of their opportunities.

Observation is also a great stimulant to practitioners, for very often the evidence challenges us, and raises awkward questions about our expectations of particular children and our professional expertise in general. If we are to take up these challenges, we have to be prepared for them with a view of learning that is well-founded in reading and experience and a willingness to learn more about ourselves and about our own professional development.

Further reading

Fawcett, M. (1996) *Learning Through Child Observation*, Jessica Kingsley Publishers, London.
Siraj-Blatchford, I. (1994) *The Early Years: Laying the Foundations for Racial Equality*, Trentham Books, Stoke-on-Trent.

For discussion

Siraj-Blatchford (1994) discusses how in-service and initial training can help us to counter the pressure of biased attitudes. She calls on us to 'recognise that educators are not objective, value-free beings. In fact, we are quite the opposite – our life-histories make us highly subjective and our actions are always value-laden' (1994, p. 150). She links observation with the ability to be self-critical and questioning as well as non-judgemental. However, being self-critical takes courage and experience.

With a colleague, arrange to get into the habit of observing each other in turn and discussing both what was observed and what was felt by the observed person. The habit of professional self-awareness helps to make questioning our practice less threatening, and the company of another equally committed person creates an ongoing dialogue which is supportive and stimulating.

7

Home and Setting Working Together

Williams was absent from school. In the middle of the morning there was a knock at the door; someone wanted the headmaster. Mr. Harby went out, heavily, angrily, nervously. He was afraid of irate parents. After a moment in the passage, he came again into school. 'Sturgess,' he called to one of the larger boys. 'Stand in front of the class and write down the name of anyone who speaks. Will you come this way, Miss Brangwen.' He seemed vindictively to seize upon her.

(Lawrence, 1915)

A child of three follows her mother along a city street towards a school. It is 1.45, and the only sound is a faint hum from the nearer classrooms. The child sees a pile of sand left in the road and drops behind to investigate it. Her mother turns to see her bending down to touch the coarse yellow builder's sand. 'You know, you've got sand in your classroom – come and see.' 'My classroom?' enquires the child. 'Yes, you remember what Charlotte said? She's going to be your teacher and we're going to see your classroom now.' 'My Charlotte came to my house.' 'Yes she did, and she played with your toys and she had a cup of tea.'

The child leaves the sand and reaches for the outstretched hand. As she goes, she says 'I like my Charlotte.'

(personal observation, London, 1988)

Collaboration and conflict

The contrast between the two scenes – the first from 1915 and the second from 1988 – is striking. Much more is now understood about the ways in which the collaboration of home and school is the groundwork of children's educational success. Yet the painful scene of 1915 must remind us that, essential as this collaboration is, it is never to be taken for granted. We have made much progress in understanding, but in fact, in spite of the gap in time, it seems as if some of the problems are still with us. We acknowledge the importance of parents' influence – three successive Education Acts of the 1980s greatly strengthened their role in their children's education. Yet there are still large areas where the hoped-for collaboration founders and communication peters out in spite of our efforts to improve the links between home and setting. Some children succeed in spite of these conflicts, but we should not underestimate the cost to them. Where the setting is working against the home in any way, children have to try and absorb the conflict themselves. 'I don't think it created conflict between parents and children so much as conflict in the children, in terms of their adaptation to the English school system' (Abrahams, 1989).

Unless we can strengthen these links we will not be able to do anything about the most intractable educational problem of our time – the 'failure to thrive' of certain pupils. This is no new problem, but one to which solutions are vital. Today, this is seen increasingly by central government as an issue that is bound up with our capacity to cope in Europe and with our competitors elsewhere in the world; from the point of view of the children and their parents, the issue is the personal development and satisfaction or otherwise of individual children and their families. Practitioners and parents working together hold some of the keys to the solution.

Underachievement has been an educational nightmare of the post-war period. Concern about its causes and remedies intensified from a growing concern for the education of the whole range of ability and background, and in particular for the inequalities in educational success which were frustrating the implementation of post-war aims for equal educational opportunities for all children.

The work of Athey (1990, for instance) has documented over a long period of time how the close involvement of parents with their children as they learn has a long-lasting benign effect on children's levels of mental activity. The fact that the improvement does not disappear when the involvement stops suggests that some lasting change may have been made in the children or in their parents – perhaps both have changed attitudes to themselves as a result of the collaboration. If this is so, here is a powerful weapon to use against the lowered self-esteem and hopelessness which can depress people's expectations of themselves and of their children. The fact that younger siblings, who did not participate, made even greater gains than the older children, suggests that the changes may have helped families to become more self-generating in their support of each other.

Pilling (1990), in her study of disadvantaged children who became relatively prosperous and successful adults, sees the essential difference as being the aims that parents had for their children. Children in the comparison group had parents who were just as committed to them, but educational ambitions were lacking. 'Not only do both parents of some comparison group members lack ambition for them, something which is very nearly absent among the educational achievers, but ambitions of the parents of comparison group members are less often educationally orientated, less specific and often at a lower level.' (Pilling 1990, p. 67)

Equal opportunities, 1963

Despite some splendid achievements in the schools, there is much unrealised talent especially among boys and girls whose potential is masked by inadequate powers of speech and the limitations of home background . . . If it is to be avoided, several things will be necessary. The pupils will need to have a longer period of full-time education than most of them now receive. The schools will need to present that education in terms more acceptable to the pupils and to their parents, by relating school more directly to adult life, and especially by taking a proper account of vocational interests . . . Finally, the schools will need strong support in their task, not least from parents, and they will need the tools for the job, in the provision of adequate staff and buildings and equipment.

(Central Advisory Council for Education, 1963, pp. 3–5)

This is a complex problem, not to be resolved by hurling insults at either homes or settings. It is one that needs to be recognized as the dangerous result of the alienation – by whatever factor – from the educational process of people who need what education can offer, and whose educational deprivation is a loss to society. It has to do with past experience and with present school procedures and with attitudes of both practitioners and parents. It can only be confronted by positive collaborative action, by adults working together on behalf of the children within a framework of mutual respect and a willingness to see the other point of view.

It is vital that every sector of education and care should consider how best to take forward the work in partnership with parents. Teaching individual children more effectively is one way to improve their life chances, but a more fundamental change, because it is more wide reaching, is brought about by changing parent and teacher attitudes. The closer parental and school aims and sympathies are, the more children are supported in their learning. This is the main hope we have of making any improvement in the biggest educational problem that we have – that of the inequality of educational outcome.

How do we tackle underachievement?

Since the early 1960s parents have been seen increasingly as having a key role in work for equal educational opportunities. A broad insight into the wholeness of the experience of education and care for young children, particularly the under-fives, has enabled us to take account of family and parental factors in our evaluation of under-fives provision. We can view the idea of early intervention in the light of the recent emphasis on the importance of provision for the under-fives being not only educational but also social and economic (see, for example, House of Commons Education, Science and the Arts Committee, 1988). The introduction of vouchers for under-fives provision in 1996 (part-time and for four-year-olds only) marked the first stage in the conversion of central government to the educational case. Its tardy acknowledgement of parental needs and wishes was, unfortunately, framed in a response which aimed to be market-driven at the expense of less well off parents; it appears, from the absence of any extra funding for playgroups, private nurseries and community provision, that it was believed that some parents would willingly choose to send their children to less well resourced settings where the in-service training and other needs of practitioners are not met.

This limited and misdirected intervention leaves much to be desired from the point of view of parents, children and practitioners, for the role that under-fives provision is called on to play is a very demanding and complex one, and much more thought and effort is required to ensure that provision is of an appropriate quality. For parents, their wishes are conditioned by their circumstances, and there are two essential circumstances to be noted by those who intend to help parents with their all-important task. The first is the economic and social context of under-fives provision; there is strong economic pressure for women to return to work after having a child, and there are also numbers of single parents of both genders. These factors are of particular importance for children under three; they are by far the most vulnerable, yet they are the group for whom there is by far the least provision. Many parents need more than a part-time place can offer – daycare as well as education. These needs must be understood as shaping parents' attitude to provision for their under-fives' education. It is also necessary to take into account that the work of early years practitioners brings them (or should bring them) into close contact with families, and with all the anxieties and stresses that they experience. In addition to the high degree of dependency in children under five, particularly in babies and children under three, many of them have to adjust to traumatic changes in their families; of the children involved in divorces at all levels of society, a high proportion – more than one-third – are under five. Practitioners who take on the task of caring for them and educating them require and deserve support for their own emotional and developmental needs if they are to provide good support for children and parents.

For practitioners, the salient point that has to be noted is that far too few of them have been appropriately trained for working with under-fives (Blenkin *et al.*, 1995) and that their access to further professional development and training is very limited. Those who work in the maintained sector are fortunate in having a time allocation for professional development, but those in private and voluntary provision do not. Practitioners in maintained education have a budget for professional development, while other practitioners do not. Practitioners working in maintained nursery schools have the support of a trained nursery headteacher and a trained deputy-headteacher, while others, including those working in reception classes, do not. Yet the quality of professional support given to children and their parents depends on the professional support given to the practitioner, and settings that are successful in their work with families give a high proportion of their time, effort and professional expertise to it. Working in a team with parents is much more complex than the term 'parental involvement' might suggest, and without respecting practitioners' needs for support it is unlikely to be successful.

Research has contributed to our understanding of the different kinds and levels of work with parents – what is meant can vary widely. The Plowden Report (Central Advisory Council for Education, 1967), which made plain the high priority that should be given to parental support for children, did not envisage parents partaking in the educational process but rather keeping in touch with classroom progress by regular visits and help with projects and outings. After the Plowden Report, however, there was a clear shift to seeing parents as educators. During the 1970s, the work of the Newsons drew attention to the parent's role as an educator. They found, for example (1977), that 82 per cent of the Nottingham parents interviewed were helping their seven-year-olds with their reading. If parents were also educators, new possibilities of collaboration would open up.

Athey's work (1990) seems to suggest that mutual reinforcement processes are at work in successful outcomes, with children's active learning being rewarded by parents who are in turn rewarded by the children's increased achievement. There were similar findings from the Child Health and Education Study (Osborn and Milbank, 1987) on the relative outcomes of different forms of provision; where parents were interested in children's progress the children appeared to do markedly better. Conversely, it might be that when parents felt much at odds with their children's practitioners, there was less encouragement for children to take advantage of what was on offer for their education. Notions of the 'cycle of disadvantage' are not discussed as much nowadays as in the 1960s. However, it is likely that educational 'failure to thrive' does have some way of passing from parent to child. Attitudes of parents which affect children's later life-chances can be affected for better or worse by relationships with practitioners, and even by whether or not settings manage to make contact with parents. Osborn and Milbank sound a very serious warning:

> 'we found large social differences in the proportion of parents who had been in touch with the staff at their child's school; as many as 43 per cent of the most disadvantaged parents had not visited the school during the previous term compared with only 14 per cent of the most advantaged parents.
>
> (1987, pp. 186–7)

The survey undertaken on behalf of the DES (Public Attitude Surveys, 1989) to discover levels of parental awareness of the National Curriculum and its assessment proposals found sharp discrepancies between different groups of parents.

Clearly, if we are going to tackle inequality in education, we need to look not just at the understandings and strategies available to us, but also at where there may be problems which both parents and staff find hard to tackle.

Tackling staff uncertainties and difficulties

To have to explain your interpretation of the curriculum in the early years, sometimes in rather contentious circumstances, to people whose dearest interests and hopes are closely bound up with what you are saying, takes courage and determination. In a context of the purely subject-based approach to education embodied in the National Curriculum it takes, above all, confidence that you are doing a good job and that you are a professional with professional attitudes, understanding and competence.

The most necessary factors of all for staff in these circumstances are a setting-wide definition of the curriculum, and support from colleagues and those in senior positions. The form the support takes may vary, but it must include the opportunity to talk about the self-doubt or frustration or confusion caused to individual members of staff, and give time for the joint working out of a group policy on the contentious issues. The one thing that must not happen to a practitioner is to find him or herself isolated and lacking support from colleagues. It is therefore a good idea to take the message about the curriculum to the parents as clearly as possible, so that the setting's general position is well established before any individual discussions begin to take place. Parents, as they talk about placing their child in the setting, need to be informed about the curriculum, and this must be followed up with regular information through meetings and written communication to keep parents in touch with the development of the setting's approach.

Communicating about the curriculum

In order to take the message about the curriculum to parents and governors or other responsible bodies practitioners need to put policies forward in clear and accessible documents. The booklet produced for parents of children in nursery schools and classes contains a statement on the curriculum which will explain the school's overall approach. Some produce statements for particular purposes, such as for open days. Parents shared in the discussion leading up to the production of one such booklet by Rachel McMillan Nursery School, London (1988). Separate booklets on specific areas of the curriculum are essential to show how the requirements of the Desirable Outcomes or the National Curriculum are being met within the setting's curriculum framework.

Another inner-city nursery school has devised a series of statements on aspects of the curriculum in which they show how their policies provide stimulating and challenging opportunities for children which are closely related to their individual stages of development. What parents can do to help is made clear.

> Many of the things we do at school can be followed up by the things you do at home. Try and provide your child with the tools to write – if paper is always available it may save those experiments on the walls!
>
> When you are out together, talk about the writing you see around you on shop fronts, adverts, road signs etc.
>
> Try and write together – make out shopping lists and write letters and cards. Have a try at making books using photos or magazine pictures.
>
> (Robert Owen Nursery School, 1989)

Communicating intentions and demonstrating the results

Communication in this case is certainly half the battle; for both parents and practitioners the other half is being able to demonstrate through the records of assessment that individual children are receiving a rich and stimulating curriculum. For parents, this is the crux of the matter, and for this reason alone assessment would be a critical area. In fact, it assumes additional importance, as will be seen below, because it is the area where parents and practitioners can, and must, work most closely together.

For the moment, however, what is at issue is how the two sets of needs may be met. For parents, the need is to see that their child's progress is being monitored and that appropriate educational provision is being made. For staff, the need is for their professional judgement to be acknowledged and accepted; being supported by colleagues communicates faith in them as professionals and concern for them as people. The two sets of needs can meet each other in clear curriculum policies and in scrupulous monitoring and record-keeping which makes it possible to be specific about the assessment of individuals. Without this, neither party is likely to be able to work together.

Working more effectively together

There are many factors and processes which contribute to building home–school links, and many ways in which parents and practitioners can move towards working together more effectively.

Success in 'parental involvement' is not built in to any one form of provision. Childminders start with the advantage of a person-to-person relationship with a small number of parents and their own perspective; similarly, day-nurseries, playgroups, nursery schools and classes, infant schools and after-school provision each have their own approach to their work with parents. It is not the kind of provision that is important, but rather the underlying principles that shape the approach. These principles help to work through the inevitable tensions of the relationship between practitioners and parents, and to find creative outcomes from them.

Smith (1980) found that there were two possible ways of looking at the practitioner–parent relationship. These she called the 'professional' and the 'partnership' models. The 'professional', as opposed to the genuinely professional, model, would be one adopted by a practitioner who took refuge in alleged expertise and wished to avoid personal contact with parents. This could happen to anyone, trained professional or not, who takes responsibility for other people's children but does not wish to take the risk involved in learning more about providing for the children from those who know them best. A genuinely professional approach to parents involves recognizing that without partnership professional expertise is not likely to be effective and is, in fact, not a valid form of expertise. All who work with young children and their parents need confidence in themselves as professionals, but this confidence must include the confidence to seek new understanding and benefit from advice from those with a particular insight. The ability to adapt to individual needs and contributions within a principled curriculum framework is a part of the practitioner's expertise which demands active effort to learn and rethink previous opinions. A professional confidence which does not include the need to learn and to develop further expertise and understanding is hardly professional.

It is the quality of these learning relationships, the 'partnership' element (Smith, 1980), which has the biggest impact on how closely parents and practitioners can work together, rather than the structure or philosophy of any particular kind of group. Some groups, such as those providing for children with special needs who are transported over long distances, or day nurseries where parents tend to be working long hours, may have less contact with parents during the working day. This does not prevent them from taking seriously parents' need to be kept informed and to have regular contact with the practitioner responsible for their children. It is the awareness of parents' needs and the willingness to be adaptable in developing ways of meeting these needs which are the most important.

Another distinction which has been made looks at things from the parents' side. If practitioners can be willing or unwilling to work in partnership with parents, parents can be divided into those who feel they are on the inside of their relationship with the setting and the practitioner and those who do not. Atkin, Bastiani and Goode (1988), who discuss the importance of this difference, describe the process as one of 'becoming familiar'. Although they find that familiar parents tend to feel more positive about the setting their children attend, it does not appear to weaken their sense of their particular role as parents.

. . . the experience tends to

- sharpen their sense of parenting, rather than blurring its distinction from teaching;
- promote a positive view of school life which nevertheless is sanguine about its weaknesses and limitations;
- serve as a stimulus to the development of home-made, compensatory strategies to tackle perceived difficulties, as they affect their own children.

Schools differ widely in their capacity and willingness to even recognise such possibilities, let alone work actively to bring about their growth and development. But there is, in our view, much untapped potential here within a rationale where parenting and teaching are brought to bear upon one another, constructively but critically. This needs to focus upon a collaboration that recognises the complementary natures and deep underlying tensions that inevitably characterise relationships between the respective institutions of home and school.

(Atkin, Bastiani and Goode, 1988, p. 59)

This is far more fundamental to children's educational success than any particular way of working together. How much involvement there is in the sense of parents working in class will vary from parent to parent, setting to setting and community to community. It usually depends on the extent to which both parties, the parents and the practitioners, can adapt to each other. The most fruitful as well as the most reliable area for working together, which is possible for most parents, is through the support of their own children as individuals. The PACT (reading) and IMPACT (mathematics) schemes, in which parents work with their children at home in a planned programme, have shown how much can be done in this way. Another area, at present little explored, is that of assessment. Here parents are often in a position to monitor progress from home and to inform teachers whether their children's learning is secure in specified areas. This kind of collaboration not only reassures parents, teachers and children that they do know what is going on; it also helps parents to see from the inside how the setting is approaching the curriculum.

Exploring the parental role

Good practice in early years settings explores strengths in the partnership with parents which should continue to be built into good practice at later stages. Many settings for under-threes, under-fives and older children inform parents in advance of proposed activities; many put up information about provision for learning during the week for parents to see, and many practitioners learn much about individual children from day-to-day conversations with parents. However, unless these processes are recorded and firmly built into the setting's procedures, there is no guarantee that they will be maintained on a regular basis or that their potential for forming and reforming what is done by staff will be exploited. Too often the informal, unrecorded event results only in inactivity; if something is happening, whether in the child's progress or the setting's provision for learning, it should be recorded, discussed and acted upon wheotherwise its value is lost. In particular, information needs to be shared with other staff and parents, and to be written down for future reference. Practitioners owe it to themselves to demonstrate their expertise in this way if they wish to be taken seriously as professionals, but they owe it most of all to the children and parents, for whom this is a once and for all experience on which much depends in the future.

Practitioners can take pride in the fact that building parents' contributions into their ways of providing for children on a recorded and established basis will link with developments in the infant and junior schools.

Merttens and Vass (1990b) have found in their examination of work on IMPACT that the involvement of parents in their children's maths education in primary schools includes:

- providing information as to proposed topics and projects so that parents can offer contributions;

- the regular sending home of books so that children can read at home;
- sending maths activities home;
- asking for parents' comments as to how the shared reading and maths work out in the home each week;
- allowing these comments to inform the teacher's records;
- welcoming parents into the classroom as helpers;
- valuing the contribution made to the child's learning by what he does at home; and
- consulting parents as well as informing them when it comes to the assessment of their child.

(Merttens and Vass, 1990b, pp. 232–3)

Not all of these activities are appropriate to nursery children and their parents, but the spirit of continuous involvement of parents most certainly is, both in the parents' informed support for the planned curriculum and in their contributions to the monitoring of their child's progress. Merttens and Vass (1990a) give examples of the IMPACT planning sheets, which are sent out to parents in advance, and of the forms for parental comments for teachers' records. Information sought for lower infant children in the form quoted is:

1. Do you think your child understands the words heavier–lighter and heavier than–lighter than? e.g. Which is lighter, a shoe or a pencil?
2. Can your child find/make two things that will balance with one another?
3. Can your child put three things in order of weight heaviest to lightest and lightest to heaviest using the balance?

(Merttens and Vass, 1990a)

Other categories of information run across the whole infant age-range.

Openness to parents

Many settings, as mentioned above, offer formalized or informal opportunities to parents to learn about their children's education and to become involved in it. Some make available general or specified statements about the curriculum offered, as mentioned earlier (see pp. 105–6). Parents need this information if they are to take part in the activities of the setting. They also need it for the monitoring of their child's progress that they will do through their own relationship at home.

Since assessment is an essential part of education there can be little doubt that parents can play an important role. Parents often contribute much to the monitoring of their children in an informal way. If this is to be effective a system is needed which will ensure that their contribution is fully documented, in order to derive the most benefit from it. Many people will be aware of how much parents contribute in informal discussions to the picture of their child that staff are trying to build up. It is helpful to be more structured about this, since there are some aspects of these very early years where parents not only help but are also able to give a lead in showing what are important experiences for their child.

Settling in: Tony

Tony visited the nursery with his parents and his little sister. It had not been possible to make a home visit since both his parents were at work during the day. He and the family looked around the room, then he settled in the home corner with his sister. At this point it was possible to talk with his parents and to find out some of the details that staff would need to know.

Record on entry

The nature of a record on entry is to enable staff to make a preliminary assessment of Tony's experiences and achievements so far, which will help them to provide appropriately for him. The record covers the family details as far as they are relevant (number and age of siblings, what languages are spoken at home, anything parents might wish to explain, such as an elderly relative living with them, etc.). It gives a picture of what Tony's experiences of care and education outside the home have been so far, and why the parents wish him to come to this nursery (this is a very good opportunity for communication about the kind of educational experiences that parents and staff believe to be important). Any relevant health factors are recorded, as are Tony's preferred occupations and anything he is nervous about – food might be mentioned, or the fact that he does not like to get messy. It will be necessary to establish who will stay with him at first, and who will bring and collect him later on – this is particularly important in the case of parents who both work full time.

The first contact with practitioners

The transition from home is the biggest step ever taken in a child's educational career; it is a real, and sometimes unnerving, landmark for the family, too. It is a time of great responsibility for staff, who need all the information and insights that parents are able to share with them. There are various ways that staff can try to make a child's early days and weeks in the setting successful, and there is a parental role in all of them. For all attempts to settle children into the setting, staff are dependent on parents to help them make a preliminary assessment of the child.

Parental support for transition and continuity

Supporting children as they move from home to a group setting makes great demands on parents. They need to be able to find their own roles as individuals.

> Not all parents can or will want to be involved in the same way: they need to find roles which they see as significant to themselves as individuals and to the benefit of their children. Many schools still have a long way to go in finding significant roles for parents or in seeing them as major resources for their children in the transition into school. Parents, like teachers, need encouragement, they need support, they often need to learn new skills, new attitudes. In the context of the present discussion [of transition and continuity in relation to the first experience of school] they may also need sheer information, not just about the school and how it operates, but about the choices open to them as parents on when or where their children may start school and the possible implications of those choices.
>
> (Watt, 1987, p. 14)

The role that a parent chooses needs to reflect the experience of the child as well as the circumstances of the parent. In the case of children who are moving between their mother tongue and that of the setting, the parent and staff have to be sensitive to the very different requirements of individual children. For some, longer parental presence is essential, while for others who have settled well the parents can help by making sure there is a home and mother tongue presence in the setting. Others prefer to see their parents engaged in, and accepted in, activities but are not keen to hear their mother tongue spoken. The kind of parental role that develops around each child's entry gives staff insight into the way the child approaches the world, and should form part of the assessment of the settling-in process.

All these positive messages about what parents can do can be continued through established procedure in existing assessment procedures, in particular the Primary Language Record. Regular records of children's progress need to be discussed with parents as much as with other staff throughout the child's time in the setting. The method of record-keeping may vary, but the sharing of records between parents and staff is essential. The informal chat at the door often contains really valuable pieces of information, such as what the child does as a result of the day's activities; these should be noted down and discussed with parents alongside information from staff later in the context of a review of progress.

The production of a book or folder about the child's time in the setting to take to the next school will be much more comprehensive and convey more information if there is a parental contribution to it.

There are ways, too, in which parents and staff can help each other with their particular understandings about what and how the child is learning. Here, difficulties may also be encountered.

Why should there by any difficulties?

While parents and teachers share an interest in the children, there are important differences in role, and difficulties in communication, which need to be acknowledged. Parents and teachers bring different perspectives and resources to this partnership, and these can on occasion cause sharp conflicts as well as bring about mutual support for the sake of the child. Hannon and James (1990) have found that parents and teachers of nursery children did not share the same approach to the teaching of reading and writing. The parents, who reported being badgered for reading and writing help at home, were concerned with teaching letter names and sounds but felt that they wanted guidance from staff as to what to do and how. The teachers were worried about parents using an unsuitable approach or putting too much pressure on the children, while play and 'pre-reading and writing activities' were so necessary for children's development. They felt that there was more to learn about literacy than letters. Whether or not one agrees that settings for under-fives should only involve children in 'pre-reading and writing' (whatever that may be defined as being it seems definitely to rule out 'real' reading and writing), what is extremely significant is that the practitioners and the parents are so far apart in their perspectives.

Recent experience, confirmed by research studies, suggests that successful collaboration between parents and their children's practitioners depends on the recognition of both viewpoints, as well as an acceptance of what each has to give. It seems that as well as the need for recognition of difference there is a desperate need for a better flow of information between the two groups.

The differences between parents and teachers are fundamentally concerned with the school curriculum. As found by Tizard *et al.* (1988) there can be much failure of communication over aims in education, and the task of reconciling the two views is not an easy one. The important point, from the point of view of this work on inner-city infant education, is the extent to which expectations can be so hard to share. Tizard *et al.* give telling figures about the extent to which teachers were unaware of what parents hoped, and how they tries to help their children at home.

> We found that the majority of teachers thought that parents, and not schools, were the main influence on children's educational success. At the same time, we had plenty of evidence that the teachers did not believe that the parents they dealt with would use this influence well. When we asked the reception-class teachers whether they thought that their parents would provide the back-up at home that they would like, only a third thought that the majority of parents would do so, and 29 per cent felt that very few, or none, would do so. This proved to be a very widespread myth amongst teachers, and certainly not supported by our evidence. At the preschool interview, the great majority of parents told us that they wanted to help with their child's education – only 20 per cent said that it was a matter to be left to the teachers. Throughout the infant school most parents were deeply committed to helping their children. In the first two years of school, 40 per cent of parents said they heard their children read five times a week. Despite the fact that very few teachers encouraged parents to help with writing and maths, a great deal of such help was being given in most of the children's homes.
>
> (Tizard *et al.*, 1988, p. 176)

In addition to the failure of communication about how much parents wanted to help their children, Tizard *et al.* found that nursery teachers took a view of the nursery curriculum that placed a different emphasis from the one taken by parents.

> Since the extent of preschool children's literacy and numeracy was so strongly related to later attainment, we tried to establish where the children had gained their knowledge. It was not possible by this stage to establish what individual school entrants had been taught in the nursery class, but in our interviews with nursery teachers we

asked them what 3R knowledge and skills they expected children to acquire before they left the nursery. Whilst there was considerable variation among the teachers, in general they put little emphasis on teaching literacy and numeracy, and their expectations in these areas were often low. For example, a third of the nursery-class teachers told us that they did not expect children to be able to count above five when they left the nursery, whereas in fact we found that the children could count to at least ten. And only a third of the nursery teachers expected their children to know the names and sounds of any letters by the time they left the nursery whereas we found that on average the children could identify five letters.

(ibid., p. 169)

This comment is very like some of the discussions that practitioners are familiar with. It would be the responsibility of the staff to balance this view with an explanation of the way in which the full range of activities are necessary for the development of children's literacy and numeracy awareness. The specialist knowledge of staff is called on to explain why play is central to mental development and creative thinking as well as to social and emotional health, and why a challenging curriculum may be expressed through the outdoor environment where children climb and run, ride bicycles and have imaginary picnics, as well as investigating the natural environment. In the battle against an impoverished curriculum the professional insights and communicative powers of staff are called on to the full.

In the case of individual children it may be very hard to explain this to a parent. One of the principle reasons for this is that, in relaxed circumstances, parents and children can derive enjoyment and benefit from quite a formal home initiation into literacy and numeracy that they undertake together. This may be completely appropriate for the home, where parents and children share so much of their experience. However, in the group setting where staff and children do not have the experiences in common that are needed to draw on, it is vital to place literacy and numeracy in a context that will be real to all the children concerned. For instance, what works most successfully in the setting, as at home, is the joint counting of apples being purchased in a shop or the joint writing of the real shopping list. Literacy and numeracy are constantly being taught in settings were children have natural opportunities to see reading, writing and mathematical thinking in operation; such children will see the point of the letters of numbers they encounter. The letters and words introduced to them in these circumstances will make sense. Settings can introduce literacy in this way without putting children in the position of being taught their letters formally; like older children. Formal introduction to the three Rs, in fact, is already undertaken much earlier in the United Kingdom than elsewhere and is rarely helpful for children. There is clearly much that each needs to explain to the other, and much to be said for the views of both parents and practitioners.

It may help to consider next how staff and parents can come to have different insights into the curriculum.

Origins of differences of view

The Hadow Report (Board of Education, 1931) described how developments in our understanding of primary education required us to lay the foundations of a new relationship with parents – one in which the nature of the young child made co-operation with the home an integral part of providing appropriate educational experiences. Yet, in the same section of the report, the committee described social and economic influences on education which exercised a powerful pull against the way in which parents had been accustomed to contribute to their children's education.

> There are doubtless several reasons why a principle so obviously sane should in practice be so often neglected. . . . In the earliest days of popular education children went to school to learn specific things which could not well be taught at home – reading, writing and cyphering. The real business of life was picked up by a child in unregulated play, in casual intercouse with contemporaries and elders, and by a gradual apprenticeship to the discipline of the house, the farm, the workshop. But as industrialisation has transformed the basis of social life . . . the schools . . . have been compelled to broaden their aims until it might now be said that they have to teach children how to live. This profound change in purpose has been accepted with a certain unconscious reluctance, and a consequent slowness of adaption.
>
> (Board of Education, 1931, pp. 92–3)

What the Hadow Report saw as 'the real business of life' had previously been learned within the community, and very largely from parents. The effects of industrialization and the consequent social developments were to make this process a thing of the past. In spite of the fact that parents, as a determining influence on the young child, must be seen as an essential part of the whole framework of the infant curriculum they were, through developments in society and changes in educational provision, being pushed to the margins of their children's educational experiences. They were no longer solely, or even mostly, responsible for teaching their children 'how to live'. If the authors of the Hadow Report saw co-operation with parents as a part of a school's provision for the educational needs of young children, they also saw that the former grounds for co-operation were being swept away. A new foundation for co-operation was required.

Conclusion

If practitioners are to have new foundations for their work, these foundations will need to consist of some of the fundamental principles discussed in this chapter. It would be impossible to avoid putting the relationship between the child and the home at the head of the list, and yet we must balance it with the practitioner as specialist. Little confidence has been shown lately in the idea of early education itself being a specialism, but we must insist on this if we are to get the quality of education we want. Equality of educational achievement may come nearer when we have more confident parents (Pugh and De'Ath, 1996) *and* practitioners sharing their understanding of the curriculum.

Further reading

Coltman, P. and Whitebread, D. (1996) My Mum would pay anything for chocolate cake! Organising the whole curriculum: enterprise projects in the early years in D. Whitebread (ed.) *Teaching and Learning in the Early Years*, Routledge, London.
Pugh, G. and De'Ath, E. (1996) *The Needs of Parents: Practice and Policy in Parent Education*, Macmillan, London.

For discussion

Pugh and De'Ath (1996) highlight four aspects of initiatives to improve home–school relations: giving information to parents and increasing access to schools, inviting help from parents in the schools, consulting parents or involving them in management, and reaching out into the community. They note also that in the past an underlying assumption of much of this work has been that parents' attitudes need to be changed by practitioners, and that therefore the contacts have tended to be on practitioners' terms.

Coltman and Whitebread (1996) describe a project undertaken to integrate school and community in which children's work focused on aspects that were shared with their families. The authors remark that there are problems with the National Curriculum in the early years and comment that an integrated, topic-based approach is most likely to secure for children the meaningful content, active participation, imaginative play and emotional security which will enhance their learning.

How far does such a project as they describe also meet the four kinds of initiatives to improve home–school relations as outlined by Pugh and De'Ath?

8

The Process of Evaluation

Why evaluate?

Today, with increasing pressure for accountability, all who are concerned with the care and education of young children are aware that some form of monitoring is called for. We acknowledge the right of various official bodies to enquire into aspects of provision for young children, and there is renewed emphasis on the rights and duties of parents to ensure that their children are being suitably provided for.

Among the many groups who take an interest in what goes on in early childhood education, the actual practitioners need to play the central role. They are the ones who make the long- and short-term decisions which determine the quality of experience received by the participating children and adults, and theirs is the ultimate responsibility for what takes place. Unless they are fully aware of what goes on in their settings, and unless they are in control of the process of monitoring and evaluation, they run the risk of having their work judged by other people's standards rather than by their own. The concerns of parents or of local authority departments are important, but we should search for ways in which to meet these concerns while retaining the freedom to develop good practice in what the setting itself aims for.

An organized group which offers care and education to young children will have all sorts of aims, intentions and commitments which underly its provision. Some will be comparatively easy to articulate – 'to provide good quality care for children while their parents are at work', or 'to offer a stimulating and enjoyable educational experience to children', for instance. However, these aims depend on judgements about what makes for good quality care and enjoyable educational experiences, and the needs of young children have to be examined in looking for ways to evaluate the setting's practice.

How can the needs of young children be defined?

From the previous chapters it will be seen that there is no particular value in trying to separate out the 'care' and 'education' aspects of early years provision. These are distinctions which at present are of importance from the funding point of view but which make little difference to the children concerned. Good quality care must involve education or run the risk of frustrating the child's constant drive to learn about the world; good quality education must care for the child in the context of the family circumstances or run the risk of separating the educational process from the child's (and the family's) social and emotional needs.

By reviewing what has been discussed so far about the needs of young children we can see some of the aspects which practitioners need to know about if they are to judge how well their provision meets requirements. Basically, it seems that the key quality of good provision lies in its responsiveness to the child's developing relationship with other people and with the world as a whole, in which the cognitive, emotional, physical and social aspects of the child's life all play a part. Because of the extreme youth of the children concerned any provision for them must embrace their home interests and relationships as well as their learning processes.

The areas of the setting's work within which practitioners can look for evidence for the monitoring process would therefore include:

- the relationships with individual children, within which monitoring and assessment take place and support and encouragement are offered for the individual and the family;
- the relationship with the home (admissions, settling in, ongoing collaboration with parents, developing a curriculum that reflects home experiences, language and culture);
- the learning environment (opportunities to explore and learn in an active way about a range of aspects of the world which includes the artistic, literary, technological, mathematical and scientific modes);
- the way in which the curriculum is developed so that it responds to children's interests and achievements (including providing resources and adult stimulus for play);
- the ways in which the adults themselves work together as practitioners and as individuals (including the team co-operation, monitoring and assessment of members of staff, the meeting of their needs as people and their career development).

Performance criteria or value-based criteria?

The need to be precise and accurate in evaluation leads to questions about how such intangible things as relationships with individual children or the responsiveness of the curriculum can be examined. There is no doubt that there are difficulties involved, but I suggest that they will tend to lie more along the lines of disagreement on the judgements about what constitutes quality and the values employed in them rather than in problems with collecting relevant evidence. This is how it should be. There is a crucial difference between value judgements and performance criteria.

There is an inherent difficulty with all performance criteria, because the choice of one factor rather than another implies a value judgement that one is more valuable than another. It is to be expected that there will be disagreements about what are the most important aspects of the setting's work, and what are the most appropriate ways to tackle them. To raise staff discussions to this level of dialogue is in fact an achievement of which we should be very proud.

To give an example, in one setting encouragement was given to parents to stay and see their children settle to various occupations when the class opened in the morning, but this led to overcrowding of the room. Discussion of the problem elicited statements of principle, such as 'The children haven't got enough room to play and they're becoming less settled, not more so,' and 'But when parents stay if they've got time in the morning it doesn't only benefit the children who are in need of a gradual settling into the class each morning, it also makes the parents feel more at ease in general. Before, they used to apologize for staying on, and seemed to feel they didn't belong there', and 'Well, you'll never get anything done until they go!'

Two different ways of looking at the relationship between home and school were being exposed in this discussion. In the first the involvement of parents at all points was seen as something to aim for; in the other the good social relationships which had been cultivated with parents were seen as existing on the borderlines of the setting's autonomy, beyond which parents should not go except with very new pupils who needed their presence for a short while. Experience with previous members of the group had shown, however, that children often were both happier and more communicative when their parents were able to spend time in the group as a matter of course, and that particular difficulties of un-settled individuals needed to be considered separately from the broad issue of parental presence in the group. After this issue had been talked over and thought about, it was easier to see what was at stake and to tackle the matter in question itself. Put more clearly in this way, it was perceived as an issue about whether to support parental involvement in the ongoing business of the group, and resolved on this basis.

The two principles, of children's need for sufficient space to play when settling in first thing in the morning, and of the importance of parents' feeling at home in the group, were not themselves seen as contradictory after the discussion. This showed that the organ-ization of the group needed to be more suited to both require-ments. Why had it been felt that parents needed to settle their children and say goodbye indoors only, when there was plenty of room in the playground? It became clear that this assumption was no longer supportable, if it had ever been, and it was then possible to see that parents and children could be welcomed outdoors as well as indoors. In fact, the extra space made it easier to talk con-fidentially with parents when necessary.

The whole issue subsequently led to a re-evaluation of the point of involving parents in the activities of the group, and to some specific suggestions for parents' participation in ways which were appropriate to their children and to their own capacities. The morning encouragement to stay continued as well; it was valuable because it was open to everyone, whereas not everyone could contribute in more specific ways.

The importance of this example is the process of development which emerged from being able to talk in detail about the way a policy was working, and this being able to establish what staff felt were criteria relevant to their work. These criteria came from ex-amining the principles of good nursery practice as they emerged from the events that were being evaluated, and were criteria of value, not of performance. This is appropriate; there are different ways of doing things in nursery work, but the underlying values remain the same. Practice can only be effectively evaluated in rela-tion to these values. Value criteria for evaluation could be dis-cussed in relation to the example given above, debated and eventually either agreed upon or kept at issue, because the oper-ation, or failure to operate, of the principles of good practice could be seen in the real situation. This perception had to be shared for any joint progress to be made, and this was dependent on having evidence of what was going on.

Collecting the evidence

To get the discussion to this point, the participants needed to be able to refer to material evidence on which they agreed. Collecting of evidence is essential for any kind of monitoring or evaluation. In work with young children, both the development of the curriculum and the assessment and monitoring of individual children, demand evidence of children's interests and levels of understanding. The role of observation is clear in both of these processes, and it is also of great important in evaluation. What unites the three processes of curriculum development, assessment and evaluation is the concern for the progress and development of the individual child and the improvement of practice in providing for this development. The three processes draw on the same observed material though they make different uses of it. To return to the subject of evaluation, each of the various areas of early years work that practitioners will want to assess will also contribute to practice in curriculum and in assessment, while drawing on similar material. The following example shows how issues arise through discussion of evidence.

Observer's record, group 1

Let us consider an example in which an observer's record is presented and discussed, and initial reactions highlight particular features which staff want to follow up. What follows is a shortened representation amalgamated from various records.

10.10.88   9.15 a.m.–11.30 a.m.

9.15
In book corner, children enter. Jane (first member of staff) talks with parents and chn (children) by door. Chn gradually filter through to tables, bringing parents. Lots of people standing by door; Jackie (second member of staff) trying to get through with clothes from yesterday to give a parent. Children chatting to each other as they explore what is put out.

   Small group standing by door to playground, discussing/competing which bike they'll have.

9.30
Children still by door; Jane involved with parent, Jackie mopping up paint spilled by departing toddler who didn't want to go.

   Children go and get coats – now six of them by door.

Screams from home corner – three chn, two pushchairs, Sarah clinging to doll Kelly wants. Alan plus friends surge over from queue by door and start 'to cook the breakfast'. Paul objects – he was cooking. Obs. (observer) tries to negotiate, persuades Kelly to let S. have doll for now if K. can have preferred pushchair. Alan etc. still surging round with an eye on the queue to go out; Paul tearful. Obs. tries talking about favourite foods.

9.45

K., S. and P. go on picnic to book corner. No room for pushchairs as other chn also present, have to leave them outside after much fuss. Squashed, even so P. goes back to home corner for 'the dinner', brings pots and pans. No room for them; also Alan appears to get them back. P. tearful again. K.: 'All right, darling, I know, we'll go to take the boat.' Moves off to brick area with S. and P. Objections by chn present; K. etc. picnic on edge of building activity.

10.00

Door opened; 18 chn go out. Room quiet. Jackie out, Jane tidies up paint area, dough table, brick area, book corner. Obs. to playground. Chn involved in dry sand tray, digging earth, climbing equipment, wheeled toys. Alan and two friends on bikes on grass, talking; A. sees obs., grins, says 'Come on, let's go' and they rush off shouting 'Ghostbusters!' K. has got S. and P. and the pushchairs in camp of blanket across A-frame, playing long story about living in woods all alone and being their Mummy. P. seems still anxious but cheers up when K. says she's going to work. He's going too. K. wants him to stay home with S. but he says S. can come to work with him and sets off. K. rather disconcerted but adapts well – 'See you tonight darling, we'll have Macdonalds when I get back'. K. spends next half-hour accumulating junk material for the Macdonalds, using the home corner and the pg. (play-ground) camp; rushes back and forth with bags of stuff. Attracts interest in hc. (home corner) and seems to be setting up shop as she serves a couple of chn. P. walks S. round pg. in pushchair; she is now his little girl and he's taking her to the park.

Alan and friends have session with Jane (adults have changed over) about giving someone else a turn on bikes. Linda and Sharon have been waiting and Jackie had warned A. etc that their turn was nearly over. A. etc. hand bikes over, turn game into running and hiding, using climbing equipment. A. catches obs.'s eye, ducks, hides, peeps out, laughs, dashes off and hides again. With friends goes into hc., obs. follows at distance. A. and friends reappear in pg. with dolls and bottles, walk round pg. saying 'We're Daddies', slightly self-conscious but seeming to enjoy it.

11.00

Obs. to book corner. 1 ch. looking at book, asks obs. what it's about. Obs. talks about book, which ch. seems to know. Jackie clearing up. Other chn join obs. and ch. (Maria). M. takes book and asks chn 'Shall I read you a story?' Obs. retires a bit. Chn sit on carpet, M. on chair. M. holds book up, tells story mostly with confidence. One ch.

waving hand, whispering 'Teacher, teacher!' M. ignores her – involved in book. Ch. v. anxious, wriggling, wants toilet. Obs. whispers 'Teacher, I think your little girl wants to go to the toilet' and M. says she can go. When ch. comes back there is some fuss about where she was sitting; M. very strict – 'Don't you sit next to her, she's a naughty girl, she's got to sit on a chair by herself.' Then 'Alright, are you quiet now, shall I go on with the story?'

11.15

Tidy-up time, chn in from pg. but Jane is happy for M.'s story to go on as chn come to book corner. M. finishes story, Jane listens.

The discussion of the observer's record

Jane began, expressing first reactions. She had no idea how long it had taken to speak to the parent, and had been wondering why the room was so noisy. She decided that she must try to get out more promptly. She was interested in the Kelly–Sarah–Paul play, as Sarah and Paul were both new (3 years 4 months and 3 years 7 months respectively) and had had a previous history of playing on their own or being very dependent on adults.

Jackie confirmed the observer's view of the playground – things were going well there in general. The effort put into encouraging investigation of the natural environment and the provision for imaginative play were both working well. There was room for continued work on the sharing of bikes but progress had been made since the last discussion about how to approach the question.

Both were rather concerned that the first 45 minutes had been so crowded and noisy in the room. Different views were expressed (see the discussion reported above) and the involvement of parents was put on the agenda for future action.

Further analysis of the record

The three participants decided that before reaching any conclusions, the record should be analysed more precisely. Rather than look for a focus which would correspond to a particular subject area or teaching aspect, the record would be looked at in terms of what it could show about the use of time, space and adult attention.

Time

The record suggested that the morning seemed to divide into two unequal parts – the time when parents were bringing their children into the room, and the time when the children were free to play wherever they liked. The lack of external structure to the main part of the morning made the first 45 minutes seem rather different. There was no set break (milk was available as and when wanted) nor was there any timed teaching spot.

Both adults working in the group felt this unstructured pattern corresponded well enough to their aim to give children as much time as possible to structure in their own way, but they wondered whether the aim for close relations with parents could be met without overcrowding the room. As was explained earlier, this was resolved by looking at the underlying assumptions to see what could be rethought.

Space

They were interested that Alan and Kelly were using both the indoor and outdoor facilities in the course of their activities, and Jackie commented that Alan seemed to benefit very much from having the extra space. His mother had remarked that over the weekends he missed being able to play outside and spent a lot of time gazing out of the window of their two-room flat. Jackie felt very pleased about the initiative with the dolls and felt that this represented a breakthrough in the presentation of interpretations of gender roles. It might link up with sharing the bikes too since several girls very much wanted to have turns.

Kelly's picnic experiences showed some problems of space when outdoor play was not available. Staff would try to make sure outdoor play was started more promptly (Jackie thought further later and suggested it should begin when the children came in) but there could be difficulties in bad weather. Making space for this kind of imaginative play was essential, and perhaps the organization of the room could be rethought to give more space; extending the home corner did not seem to be the answer as the children had specifically sought a new spot for the picnic. The book corner was not suitable when it was being used for reading and listening to tapes, but the brick corner did seem a logical place, in that necessary features such as boats or islands or new houses could be constructed there.

Adult attention

Jane said that the morning had been rather unusual because the parent who had needed her attention for a long time had an urgent problem to explain. There seemed no obvious way to deal with this differently. Jackie said she had felt very frustrated by the paint accident, which was right by the door where people were coming in and had prevented her being with the children in the other part of the room. She had felt uncharitable towards the toddler's parent, which was silly, as this sort of thing was all part of the work and at least it showed the toddler wanted to come to nursery. She would make sure that anything messy was well away from the door next time and would station herself at a distance from the door when she was not on welcoming duty. The one not welcoming could take children outside, or if the weather did not allow, should be involved with the children indoors.

Both adults commented that they were rather struck by how little they appeared to say or do in the record. Was the observer sure things had not been missed out? The observer explained that the focus had been very much on the children, particularly out of doors and that adults were noted if they were in contact with children being observed. Jane commented that tidying up after most of the children went out at about 10.00 a.m. had taken rather a long time, and was another good reason to avoid overcrowding the room. The observer had picked up the adults' interventions about sharing the bikes, and Jackie had been involved in several conversations and games with individual children in the playground. They might consider whether a different approach to tidying up would give more time to spend with the children.

Conclusions about the record

Some areas gave satisfaction to the team, some gave cause for concern. The areas of concern would be followed up, some by action and others by further investigation. The timing of the outdoor play would be changed at once, and a further observation made after a week or so to see how things had altered. It would probably be possible to tell from staff impressions whether the pressure on space was sufficiently improved.

The organization of the indoor space needed to be improved. With the winter coming and large numbers of new children entering staff wanted to be as ready as possible to meet their needs, and children like Paul and Sarah were easily upset by having to compete with older children.

The freedom of adults to respond to children was a very important issue – it would be sad to be so busy tidying up that there was not enough time to play and talk. Before reaching any hasty decisions it would be worth another investigation to see whether there was any cause for anxiety. This time staff would use a tape recorder, taping one person one morning and the other the next. This could be repeated until a sufficiently clear pattern emerged.

In each of these three issues the staff wanted to involve the observer again once their own next steps had been made.

The pattern of evaluation

This example shows a cyclical pattern of processes. The initial information leads to an analysis of evidence from which some statements are made about what are perceived to be problems. The grounds on which these are seen to be problematic relate to the sort of performance criteria discussed earlier, which may vary somewhat between professionals but which are capable of being argued about and compared in terms of certain values.

Once these particular problems are identified they can be attended to, and the results investigated to see what improvements have been made. The cycle continues, giving staff the chance to evaluate by various means the impact of what they do on their professional performance, and then to identify problems, decide what to do and take action again. At each part of the cycle staff are able to reflect on the criteria involved in the quality of their performance and to take the initiative in the discussion and definition of these.

The aim of evaluation should be not just to find out how well staff are doing what they set out to do. It should help staff to notice what it is that they are doing which they did *not* set out to do – the hidden curriculum may become a bit easier to see. Evaluation will also enable staff to ask questions about what it is they are setting out to do – to provide a critique of practice. Unless evaluation fuels and guides this kind of critique it is only capable of endlessly rubber-stamping the initial plans of the evaluators. Attention to the experiences and intentions of the children in the group will provide outside information to enable practitioners to take a step back from their work so that they can get a broader perspective.

Supporting the evaluators

Evaluation can seem a rather threatening experience. It is perhaps reminiscent of those terrifying teachers of one's youth who asked to look at one's book in class, after which all one's weaknesses and wickednesses were exposed and castigated. Certainly evaluation should have regard to the sensitivities of those concerned, and it should be understood that it is being undertaken in a professional spirit, with the intention of furthering the practice and development of members of staff. It should also be emphasized that this kind of evaluation is self-evaluation and therefore under the control of the staff.

Evaluation is a natural and essential part of the professional relationship with young children. Being professionally self-critical is fundamental to developing good standards of work, and should add to professional self-confidence. 'In a nursery where action is determined in this way, all staff should be refining their skills (the more closely you look at something, the more information you are likely to gain), growing in confidence and becoming better able to withstand uninformed criticism and the whims of society' (Dowling, 1988, p. 140).

Evidence and criteria for judgement

Each of the different processes outlined above contributes to evaluation in particular ways, but evidence is the foundation of the sequence of processes. Evaluation consists of collecting evidence, reflecting on it, noting particular patterns as they emerge, and trying to see what principles of good practice are involved.

From this sequence, there will emerge certain issues that are seen as being of importance. In the example given above, there emerged the two issues of the children needing enough room to play and the necessity for parents and staff to be in contact. These issues provide the criteria for decisions about what is the best way to do things.

Relationships with individual children

Discussion of individuals' progress is doubly valuable – for each individual, and because it leads on to the review of the coverage of the whole class, the type of evidence available, what action is taken, how effective it is. Value judgements which emerge from this process can point to the criteria for good practice. For instance, a child who causes concern may show the need for more and different information – 'Could we ask for a home visit to talk about things? We really ought to have home visits for every new child' – which points to criteria of closeness to the home and of adequate information on which to draw. Or there may be a question of how to treat social issues – 'I think he and Michael are using those bikes to avoid having to co-operate with the other children – they're always on them, and seem to have established that they have first choice'. This suggests the need for guidance to children on how to take turns without losing face, and expresses the idea that this behaviour will be seen subsequently as a criterion of success when it is achieved after the problem has been identified. Each child's progress or difficulty can point to processes or practices in the nursery as functioning well or less well.

Relationships with the home

The experience of individual children provides the key to evaluation: are there children who have difficulty with parting from or greeting their parents? Are there parents with whom it is hard to make contact? This is an opportunity to check that the curricular focus, the activities, the reading materials, the displays, reflect what is known and familiar in the child's home experience. Whether it is a new baby or a grandparent lately arrived, this needs to be part of the setting's work because it is part of the home. In the same way, bridges to the home must be built with objects and materials, pictures and music, spoken and written languages that have their own place in the setting because of their place in the home. The criteria that spring from these principles of practice should underly decisions in planning for the future. They will also be referred to when staff consider what to do about problems as they arise.

The learning environment

The range of potentially valuable educational experiences is virtually endless, and it seems counter-productive to engage in a checklist approach, which might lead one to try to dissuade a child from a preoccupation with, say, drawing simply because she had not yet completed a model. Adults have a responsibility to ensure that there is a suitably wide range of opportunities available on offer all the time so that children are able to choose, and to make genuine choices. Practitioners will develop criteria not just about the provision of, for example, musical instruments but also the positive inclusion of them by staff in their activities so that children are drawn to the instruments and supported and guided in their use of them. Any criteria here will link with evaluation of the curriculum and its development, since the learning environment is, as described earlier, one way of constructing the curriculum. Evidence can be collected about what children choose to do, which seem to be the preferred activities, what areas of experience staff feel least confident about providing. Certain areas may be seen as less important than others: 'I think you ought to stay indoors and do some drawing before you go outside' suggests that the potential of outdoor play for social, scientific, imaginative and physical development is being valued less highly than more academic-looking activities done with pens at tables. If staff were trying to discuss the issue of drawing being seen as work and outdoor play as relaxation, the criteria they would refer to would be the principle of children's need to learn through play and vigorous activity as well as through writing and other pursuits associated with academic work.

The way in which the curriculum is developed

Here, evaluation can draw on the evidence of children's interests to see how far the plans are capable of responding flexibly and encouraging children to go further. This asks staff to seek evidence of children's experiences and of what they do in the setting, and to look at the way in which they themselves try to develop a responsive curriculum. The arrival of the workmen to dig up the road provoked a resurgence of awareness of things that could be under the ground; children dug pits in the playground, buried 'treasure' in the sand tray and peered down the sink. All of this intense mental activity was marginalized, quite unintentionally, until understanding of the imaginative, scientific and technological potential dawned on the staff. An opportunity like this does not occur every day, but there are many small opportunities to develop a curriculum that focuses on the intellectual content of children's real and meaningful experiences. Everything that is undertaken in the group can contribute to children's learning; seeing children's pictures being sorted to be taken home caused Murtaza to ask why his pictures were never at the front, but always towards the back. After explanation about alphabetical order, he explored the significance of this, and would help other children to find their pictures as he built up his sense of the order of their names in the alphabet. The decision to give time specifically for this process was based on the criteria of relevance and cognitive content in the curriculum.

The ways in which the adults themselves work together

The members of a setting's team will have their own sense of criteria for judgement, often focusing on factors like communication between members and on the provision for each to develop his or her own particular gifts and expertise. They can even discuss the process of evaluation itself; does it take too long? Does it seem to cover all the important areas? Is eveyone getting a chance to contribute? The process of evaluation can itself be evaluated in the light of the criteria of good practice.

Conclusion

There is no set path for evaluation, because what practitioners do is dependent on what they think is important about their own work, and on what the children, parents and other members of the team bring. Complete agreement between members of a team is unlikely; it is unlikely between teams, about every aspect of their work, or about how it is best achieved. Where the participants are able to share information about what happens in their setting and about how children experience it, they are then able to talk about the values underlying their work, values which guide them in the way they use their professional skill.

Further reading

Robson, S. and Smedley, S. (eds.) (1996) *Education in Early Childhood: First Things First*, David Fulton in association with the Roehampton Institute, London.

For discussion

Robson, in 'The physical environment' (in Robson and Smedley, 1996), proposes that practitioners should 'take a long hard look' at the space that is available, indoors and outdoors. They should make a plan of the space, with fixed points and equipment noted. Then they should consider their aims for the children, their views on learning, and the range of experiences they want the children to have, before trying to draw up plans for the space which take account of these factors (p. 163). She identifies a further stage of reflection, in which practitioners can ask themselves whether the environment supports children in their efforts 'to feel a sense of belonging, and to feel safe' and 'to represent their experiences in as many ways as possible' (p. 165). She continues the list of questions through linguistic development and development as readers and writers, through aesthetic and expressive development, social development, moral and spiritual development, mathematical development, physical development, scientific development and technological development.

With a colleague, discuss how far these categories correspond to your aims for children. When you have decided on your own personal list of priorities, undertake the kind of audit of space indoors and outdoors that Robson suggests. Then try to plan for your aims within the constraints of the space, fixed points and equipment. When you have implemented your plans, undertake observations regularly each day to establish how well children are able to take advantage of your plans. Use your list of priorities to make judgements about whether the plans are appropriate and the available space is sufficient for the children's needs. Discuss your observations with your colleague and compare notes on your conclusions.

9

Improving the Education of Young Children

In the search for the key to high-quality educational provision for children under the age of eight we need to isolate some of its vital qualities. We have seen that the response of the adult to the child is very important, as is the understanding of how children learn, and an awareness of the intellectual background on which we draw to support and extend children's learning. Now we can summarize the way in which these ideas are drawn into a coherent structure in the British early childhood education tradition.

What is the early years curriculum?

The tradition of education for the early years is that it should be based on understanding of the way in which children learn. Meeting the needs of young children for freedom to play and to explore, working to build close relationships with their parents, and drawing on what is thought to be the best of the knowledge, skills and understanding of the world that could be offered to such young children – all these make up the essence of the curriculum. Many outstanding people have contributed to it and we build on what they have already laid down.

Although there are very great differences between children at different stages of the years between birth and eight, there is a continuity of characteristics of learning which gives good quality early childhood education unity and coherence. These characteristics may be summed up as follows:

- the value placed on contacts between people;
- the value placed on learning through personal choice of activity;
- the value placed on practitioners and children working in partnership.

These characteristics give us ideas about how to improve educational provision for children under eight.

Whatever the curriculum content and activities thought suitable for a particular stage, young children learn in contact with other people: parents, practitioners and other children. The quality of relationships is crucial in provision for them, and in the working co-operation between staff and parents. The partnership between parents and practitioners in the education of the very youngest children is essential if the first steps in a setting outside the home are to be a success. Practitioners can scrutinize their practice and the setting's policies to see what value is attached to children's social and emotional needs, and they can make decisions about what may need to be changed in order to provide for children. If the answer to a criticism is that the curriculum and its assessment demand that children work on their own, or it seems that the practitioners and parents are not making contact effectively, then perhaps the interpretation of the curriculum or the methods of assessment should be changed so that children can work together and parents can help them at home.

Young children are active and independent players and thinkers, who learn from handling real materials, objects and situations and through their own spontaneous exploration, representation and play. If, instead, we are told that whole class teaching is more effective, and that play is for when the work is satisfactorily completed, we ought to question what it is that children are being trained for that is more important than their emotional and intellectual development.

The adults who work with these children have to plan and provide the setting for them, and then to adapt their provision to enable the children to further their learning in the way that best suits them. The children's education becomes, in the most successful cases, a shared concern between children, parents and practitioners. If it seems that practitioners are only valued as deliverers of set packages of subject content, we should ask whether such young children are being educated and cared for or merely produced to a predetermined blueprint which takes no account of human variations and individuality. We might also point out that no blueprint laid down in the 1980s and 1990s is likely to be much use in the next century.

Early childhood education and quality criteria

There is much 'education' for children under eight that is more like drilling, in which children are prepared to be passive recipients of instructions who will carry out what they are told without questioning their orders. Children of two are, in some settings, already following a timetable of lessons and using worksheets. Practitioners and parents, impressed by the multitude of documents and pronouncements issuing from central government and OFSTED, are accepting lower standards of consideration for children's emotional, social and physical needs, especially in reception classes. What is more, under the guise of raising standards, children are being dissuaded from using their brains to question and shape their educational experiences, and are being prevented from developing their powers of communication because of the weight of the timetable at Key Stage 1. We need to have some criteria for what is good practice to refer to, and these can be based in early childhood education.

Early childhood practitioners provide education through planning based on observation and through a resource-based environment for exploration and play. This approach meets the requirements for a wide and rich network of educational processes and understandings within which children can develop their ideas and capacities for present achievement and enjoyment, as well as lay the foundations of their future education. The quality of the curriculum depends on the extent to which it is linked with observation and assessment. Record-keeping ensures that the adults do not lose track of the children's activity and ideas.

Nursery education, although severely hampered by a lack of resources, has managed still to be the source of some most important insights into what constitutes good-quality education for young children. As Clark (1988) has pointed out, there are many promising avenues for future exploration through research, initial teacher education and in-service training. At a time when the impact of the National Curriculum must be taken into account, it is particularly important to follow up indicators towards good practice which emerge from research of all kinds. Some interesting possibilities are explored below (see pp. 142–3).

What services are included within the term 'nursery education'?

What is meant by the term 'nursery education'? Where it is used to describe a part of the maintained education service, it cannot be used to describe all the different kinds of provision that may be made for children under five in schools or in any other institution or group. Nursery education is a specialist education service which provides for children between the ages of three and five years. It is provided in local authority nursery schools and in nursery classes attached to infant schools. The admission of four-year-olds to reception classes, or the encouragement of employers to provide private nurseries, does not mean that the government has discharged its commitment to the education of the under-fives.

Principles of nursery education – the search for quality

Nursery education, not as local authority provision but as an educational philosophy, is relevant to provision for the under-fives wherever they are. The key to nursery education lies in the principles of the nursery curriculum, staff training and ratios, and in the accommodation, resourcing and equipment of the nursery setting. The dialogue about the needs of under-fives – the 'nursery' children – takes place on the grounds defined by reference to their needs for care and education, or, as David (1990) puts it, 'educare', since the two are not to be separated. The issues which form the matter of the dialogue are wide ranging and have implications for providers of private and public services for under-fives. They are also relevant to the work of infant teachers.

The nursery curriculum and the 'basic skills' – drawing attention to the child's real achievements

The nursery curriculum aims to support children's all-round development. It should not be seen as an introduction to what are called 'basic skills', by which is often meant such competences as being able to trace or copy precisely. There may be a place for such an activity but it is the child's intention in what is done that is seen as important. An example (p. 138) may illustrate what is meant.

What will happen to nursery education?

The relationship between nursery education and the National Curriculum is at present rather uncertain. Nursery schools and classes are not the only educational setting where a nursery curriculum is needed. This is because of the large numbers of four-year-olds who

Tony (4 years 6 months) watched a label being written and stuck to the back of a ringbinder for children's records. He asked what it was for, what it said and why you had to label binders. After the explanation he went to the drawing table and cut a thin rectangle of paper of similar dimensions, on which he drew a line that zig-zagged up and down like writing. He then offered it to me, and when I asked what it was for he said 'It says "It's Vicky's book"'. I stuck it on the back of another ringbinder. The next day he arrived with a bus ticket and went straight to the drawing table, reappearing later with a careful facsimile which he showed to me before going outside to organize a bus service. He did not have quite so exacting an approach to the later tickets that he made, but the point had been established with the first one, as with the label on the ringbinder; he could make something that would fulfil a genuine purpose in the classroom.

He certainly was developing several basic skills, such as using scissors and pens, holding them in the most effective way for himself, cutting to a particular size and shape, moving the pen from left to right as our culture writes, observing and reproducing the different letter sizes and outlines, and copying exact numbers and letters in their order and distribution on a small piece of paper. There is no doubt that these are all good skills to have, and that a rich curriculum would stimulate children to practise these skills, particularly in the course of imaginative play. However, if asked which was the more important, to be able to copy individual letters or to know that literacy is essential for the organization of one's life and how one can use it even as a small child, there should be little hesitation. People who can exercise the basic skills – who have been drilled in them for most of their years of compulsory schooling – form a very large proportion of the early school-leavers who so concern us nowadays. The essential skills of literacy, mathematics, science and all the other disciplines are learned more easily and more permanently when they are learned in a context that makes sense to the learner.

are in infant reception classes despite being under age. Their teachers are not able to provide a separate curriculum for them, in spite of the fact that their age should entitle them to nursery education.

Those who are concerned for the under-fives in infant classes (there are nearly 2000 three-year-olds involved) must sympathize with their teachers as they try to meet their obligations to the older children under the National Curriculum and at the same time care for the needs of the younger children in the class. What is involved in providing for the under-aged children has been documented by Pascal and Ghaye (1988). They point out, for instance, the significance of work on mismatch between task and learner in school. The conclusion is that when teachers provide for the learning of a group of children they pitch their provision at a notional average child. When the class includes four-year-olds this is 'an inadequate and seriously inhibiting view of what is involved in planning an enhancing and truly facilitating curriculum for these children' (Pascal and Ghaye, 1988, p. 5)

Some of these younger children may have both teachers and nursery nurses; they may even – if they are lucky enough – have a nursery nurse and a teacher who has been trained for the three- to eight-year-old age range. However, many children do not have either. This situation calls for an awareness of the need for the nursery curriculum in infant schools where under-fives are admitted. This need should be recognized, even if it is initially difficult to envisage this approach co-existing with the introduction of the National Curriculum. It is to be hoped that in-service training, with better staffing, resourcing and support, will enable teachers and nursery nurses to find the ways in which a good curriculum for nursery-aged children can help to support a good curriculum for older children as well.

As a result of the introduction of the Desirable Outcomes, there may be pressure to extend the approach of the National Curriculum into provision for the under-fives – to extend programmes of study into nursery provision under the guise of preparing children more effectively for infant school. What are the implications of this? Practitioners will wish to ask how it is envisaged that programmes for older children will assist younger ones. They will need to be able to demonstrate the progress that children are making through having a curriculum designed for them, instead of a handed-on set of programmes. Parents in particular will need full information, both about their own children and about the nursery curriculum in general, to enable them to make up their own minds about this development. Parents need to be helped to make a most important distinction. Nursery education can play a fundamental role in children's present and future educational success, but its criteria of success are related to the children's present achievements and development. There is no place in nursery education for preparation for any later stage, except in terms of the enjoyment and enrichment in education which is a good preparation for life itself. The nourishment offered to children today is for their benefit today; good food now certainly makes for stronger children later, but the food must be appropriate for today. You cannot prepare for a later stage of education by anything but a fully appropriate educational diet now.

Helping with infant assessment

The way in which nursery education can make a contribution to later stages of education can be illustrated by looking at the difficulties infant schools will face in trying to implement the requirements of the National Curriculum without a sound basis of nursery education on which to rely. The result of this neglect of the under-fives is that so disparate are children's experiences before the age of five that many infant teachers will have great difficulty with the assessment process central to the functioning of the National Curriculum.

If well-resourced nursery education were widely available this situation would not be so difficult for infant teachers. High-quality educational provision for the under-fives enriches and develops children's natural learning so that many of the problems seen in infant schools and later are much less likely to occur. The time spent in infant education is insufficient to make up the ground lost by missing out on nursery education, as well as keeping up with the first years of compulsory maintained education.

Again, quality in nursery education is based on continuous assessment of individual children's progress, and offers to hard-pressed infant teachers a view of how assessment under the National Curriculum can be carried out without restricting children's learning. In addition to this general benefit, individual children who have had a good nursery education arrive at their reception class with their assessments already under way. Records of achievement over the years in nursery schools and classes should be available to infant teachers, who can judge what benefit children have derived from the educational experiences they have been offered and can build appropriately on them.

There can be no doubt that the professional expertise of nursery trained staff has an enormous amount to offer practitioners working with older children because of the requirement for assessment and record-keeping that the Education Reform Act brings with it. If this is to be successful in the infant stage it needs to depend on sound records of children's progress from the nursery stage so that infant staff can see what a child is building on and how best to help.

Nursery practitioners have their own interpretation of the curriculum as it arises from their interactions with children. They can also explore the implications of exchanges with children of other age-ranges for their own provision of educational experiences, and gain the stimulus of a new look at the ideas about learning, and about knowledge and understanding of the world, which are the essence of education. They have much to give as well as much to gain from this exchange.

Improving provision for the under-fives

There was a warm welcome for the thoughtful and wide-ranging report of the House of Commons Education, Science and Arts Committee (1988), which pointed to the contribution that education can make to the development of the under-fives. The committee stated that there is an urgent need for a steady expansion of nursery education, and for the provision of high-quality training for sufficient numbers of nursery teachers and nursery nurses. The committee indicated that it recognized that the quality of the educational aspect of the provision is the key ingredient, whatever the setting, for the under-fives. It may not be convenient or politically acceptable, but it is vital to maintain this principle at a time when the already wide-ranging forms of provision are changing rapidly in response to the perceived need for women's work outside the home.

The failure in the United Kingdom to expand nursery education over the past 20 years has meant that many children have not benefited from what has for so long been recognized as the appropriate high-quality educational experiences for the under-fives. We need to give a high priority to the educational aspects of provision for young children, and to recognize the potential role of nursery education in this. Although the expansion planned in the 1970s did not occur, insights from good practice in nursery education have contributed to the development of a range of initiatives in providing for the under-fives. Such insights continue to contribute to the evolution of criteria for the assessment of provision. We need a planned future for nursery education within the wider spectrum of provision for children from birth up to the age of compulsory education. In addition, we need to ensure that nursery education is made available on a more consistent basis both as a service to children and as a resource for other forms of provision.

The development of centres of excellence based on nursery schools and centres would enable us to focus on areas where investment is most needed – provision for under-threes and support for their practitioners, and partnership with parents.

As long as they have some kind of place to go to, does it matter what it is?

It matters enormously what kind of provision the under-fives experience, for two reasons. There is the need for quality of education as the foundation for young children's successful learning, as well as the need for high-quality provision that is responsive to the social realities of families. The guidance that we can get from nursery education about educational quality needs to be linked with an examination of the many other factors to be taken into account, in particular the strengths and weaknesses of different strategies for meeting the needs of children and families.

In her recent review of research in provision for children under five, Clark (1988) has pointed to what she feels are some of the outstanding issues. During the period of her investigations the position has changed from the expansion of nursery education in the 1970s to a situation in which it was appropriate that her remit should be children under five rather than under-fives' education, since the latter had so immediately come under pressure. The many different kinds of provision which now exist need to be evaluated for what they can offer to people in different circumstances.

Areas for future exploration

Several areas outlined by Clark (1988) cry out for further investigation, each of them promising to tell us more about how we can improve what we do for the under-fives. It is vital to realize that families and children have different needs, and that high-quality provision will need to come in different forms which are sensitive to the needs of the people who use it. It will be necessary to look again at some preconceived attitudes to the home's influence, to parents and to their role today. The emphasis on making up deficiencies in the home, which was the focus of the compensatory education of 20 years ago, needs to be readjusted; we need to look at children's behaviour in more than one context before we can say whether or not children have deficiencies. We need also to examine how children think, and how aware they are of their own thinking processes; for instance, knowing *what* you do not know is often better than knowing *that* you do not know. Children are aware of memory, and two-year-olds will sometimes say 'I don't bemeber it'. Later, children may complain that someone has not responded as they expected: 'I asked her and she said not to'. A child explaining to another child how to do something may be reduced to showing the movements, not explaining the reasons for them. The normal daily interactions of a group of children with their adults are full of this sort of opportunity for learning about the world, about other persons and about thinking, but they need to be taken up seriously. The adults need to plan how to support the child who wants to explain but cannot do so, or the child who cannot understand another person's motives.

Maintaining and developing quality

Linking up with children as they investigate the world around them, and indeed as they think about thinking, demands a lot of the adults involved in supporting them. Nursery education can offer experience in constructing a curriculum which fits. This curriculum, derived from an assessment process that is based on observation, has been identified by Clark (1988) as one of particular importance, and it is a conclusion from her review of educational research to which we should pay particular attention. It is extremely demanding for adults, and may be too onerous without adequate professional support. There may be a link here with some other findings which associate children's progress more with nursery schools than with nursery classes.

The report of the House of Commons Education, Science and Arts Committee (1988/9) has indicated that it sees good practice as occurring both in nursery classes and nursery schools. However, recent work (Osborn and Milbank, 1987) has warned that there may be reason to watch for more difficulty in reaching high standards in nursery classes, perhaps due to the lack of nursery colleagues' support. We need further research on this, to see what factors may be involved. Whatever may ultimately be decided about this, there is no doubt at all about the crucial role of nursery schools and centres, both as centres of excellence and as the trainers of the practitioners of the future. Policy-makers at national and local levels must include them in their planning for the future of services for the under-fives.

Research and young children

The role of research in the development of provision for the under-fives must continue, and be expanded. This is too important an age-group for its educational future to be left to chance; researchers need to find out just what it is that practitioners are doing with their groups, and staff need to find out what researchers can tell them about evidence of how children learn most successfully. This is, of course, vital for the children, and for the parents. It is also extremely important for the professional development of the staff themselves, for two reasons. The first is that every professional person needs to investigate and evaluate how well they are doing the job; this is in the interests of the people for whom they professionally assume responsibility – in this case the children and parents. The second reason has to do with the professional obligation to evaluate work with children in order to know how to develop the curriculum – staff cannot know what to do next until they know how successful they have been so far. Research has, therefore, much to offer nursery staff.

However, there are certain problems associated with research, the main one being the question of how to establish links between the researchers and the staff in settings. There is an understandable feeling that research is too rarified for the daily business of looking after children – that its conclusions are better suited to the readers of learned journals than to nursery teachers and nursery nurses. But is this really true? Can we afford for it to be so?

We very much need to know how children learn in groups in order to give them the best possible educational start. It is most important that the education of young children should be researched. We need to examine the issues connected with their education, and nursery staff should be counselled in how to use research findings in an informed way. In particular we need to focus on in-service education for early years practitioners. This in-service education should include curriculum development and assessment, in which a wide range of staff could be involved.

Staff should be supported to monitor progress from home to nursery to infant education. This requires the monitoring of continuity and change in the child's educational environment as well as establishing continuity with the home. The heightening of professional skills that is required is best done in a research partnership where observations need to be sharply targeted and assessments focused. The high quality and close focus of recent research, such as Hughes' work on numeracy in nursery-aged children (1983), would be an important and inspiring model for good practice by nursery staff who were getting to know their children's levels of understanding. The value of different kinds of play provision needs to be examined urgently as must children's dependence and independence in class. Above all, staff must know more about how the web of personal relationships in a group may be made more sustaining to individual children, and what it is that can cause the web to allow some children to fall right through or even to feel strangled by what should support them. There are pointers in those research perspectives which analyse the conversational exchanges of parents and children and of staff with the same children, and teachers must have help in order to become sensitive to what may be going on in their own groups. Staff themselves need support and challenge, as well as training in a high level of organization to monitor these vital aspects of their work.

But can the apparently neutral and withdrawn stance of the researcher be translated into a classroom reality? Can research be concerned with such seemingly minor details as practitioners encounter every day?

What does research have to do with daily work?

One could put this the other way round, and say that research ought very much to concern itself with the daily work of practitioners. What could be more important than the ways in which decisions about education are reached? The work of outstanding researchers has shown how the apparent minutiae of education are like the tiny pieces which make up a mosaic – each one must be right for the purpose or the whole design is lost. The analyses of conversations at home and at school that Wells has presented (1987, for example) show how each brief exchange of words is worthy of attention for its educational potential. Barrett (1986) shows how the smallest organizational details of the early stages of education have an effect on children's views of themselves as learners. There is in fact a noteworthy body of research which already concerns itself with the daily experiences of young children in various forms of provision. What is required next is for staff to feel less reticent about adopting the attitude of researchers themselves.

The research stance to the classroom is not in fact alien to staff who adopt the observation-based approach to assessment and curriculum development. In reality what they are doing when they commit themselves to this approach to education is researching the behaviour and development of their children. This is why what they discover contributes such a well-founded justification for their work, and why the professionalism of staff is so much enhanced by this process.

What can nurseries offer to researchers?
By observing, recording and reflecting, practitioners can have access to much of the kind of detail that researchers use every day. Moreover, researchers will need to work with practitioners if they wish to develop their insights into what makes for good educational provision. There are as many different ways of researching groups as there are groups in existence. What is indispensable is that the staff involved should be able to draw on a sound practical and theoretical base for this work. The foundation of nursery decision-making on observation – on evidence, not on preconceived notions – means that there exists here a conceptual and practical framework into which research proposals from outsiders can fit smoothly.

Which issues should we be researching?

Clark (1988) points to many potential areas of research which would be of great interest to anyone who wishes to provide well for the education of the under-fives. The evidence from existing research in children's language, through the use of radio-microphones in the home, shows that practitioners must think carefully about the places and the way in which they talk with children; the language is often richer at home, with peers or in contexts where activities with adults make human sense. It is important that the role of adults is sensitively structured with the meaning for children as the top priority.

Of the vital issues still under-researched, many practitioners – in infant as well as under-fives' education – would agree with Clark (1987) that continuity of educational experience from three to seven or eight years of age is of great importance. So far, only studies of transition have been undertaken; Barrett's work (1986), for instance, focused on one continuum, that from home to school. We now need evidence on the continuity which is challenging but not stressful for young children. There would also be much interest in knowing more about the different levels of literacy and maths awareness in young children. This should include awareness of early fluent readers both so that we could support them and so that we could learn what factors helped them. We could then help other children, too.

Staff in nurseries and reception classes would like to know more about the development of children who are bilingual, and about the effects of staff speaking the mother tongue. The astounding achievements of such young children in mastering more than one language when they have only just become proficient in their own deserves recognition and investigation; Tasneem, mentioned earlier (see pp. 92–3) spoke Gujarati and Hindi in addition to English. Again, some children grow up speaking more than one language from the first; this is also worthy of investigation in its own right, and may have much to teach about second-language teaching in later stages.

Developing a critical attitude to research

The aim is not simply to inform staff by teaching the findings of research. Staff must be able to watch for selectivity in research: to ask why there were no bilingual children in certain studies, for instance, and to be confident in evaluating the consequences of any findings for their own work.

What researchers will need to provide

Staff have a right to ask that research with which they are concerned should take a form that they can work with. They will find that there is a body of research which concludes that making research with practitioners successful implies going about it in a particular way. Researchers themselves will find that their proposals need to take account of certain desirable qualities if they are to be acceptable to classroom practitioners. These correspond to certain aspects identified by researchers with experience in action research. For instance, Bruner (1980) stipulates that research should be genuinely participatory if practitioners are to consider it relevant to their practice – they must feel that they are sharing in the work, albeit with a different role. This would certainly imply that they are in sympathy with the aims of the research, and Stenhouse (1975, pp. 161–2) adds that the research should be supportive of their own intentions. Openness to practitioners' initiatives is a quality sought by many writers, including Bruner (1980) and Elliott *et al.* (1981), and this is important because of the opportunity it offers to develop and enhance the professionalism of the practitioner.

This brings out the most essential quality of this kind of collaborative research – that research should increase the professional expertise of the practitioner. This kind of development accords with the view taken by Stenhouse (1975), that educationalists should aim towards an extension of the professionalism of the practitioner and push out the boundaries in many directions – towards other disciplines as well as towards their own professional development. In the case of a multidisciplinary nursery, the staff disciplines would be enhanced but in addition the large number of other relevant disciplines would also add to the practitioner's expertise.

The foundation of this sharing of the research lies in the social relationship between researcher and practitioner, which must be strong enough to hold fast the bridge between different roles and perspectives. Bruner (1980) mentions the need to keep time free for listening to individuals. In his Oxford Preschool Research Group publication (1980) there are instances of practitioner and researcher perspectives; in particular, the contribution made by MacMahon illuminates the link between social behaviour and research aims. Just as in a personal, non-professional relationship there must be some degree of parity of initiative between participants if the needs and concerns of each are to be recognized, in this kind of research the co-operative goals demand that neither side has exclusive control of the agenda. Each participant must leave space for the other's initiative, and the eventual structure must be the result of negotiation, whatever the level and nature of each participant's contribution.

Starting out in the setting

Researchers cannot come with a prepared notion about what the setting will be like. The fact that no classroom is like another means that researchers need to employ a variable sensitivity as a part of their research equipment. The agenda prepared in advance is not possible in this kind of research. If research in nursery education is to be successful, it will need to be collaborative from the outset although the different roles of the participants must be recognized.

This kind of co-operative action research should not be conceptually very difficult once the new roles of researcher and practitioner have been accepted. The negotiation of focus between researcher and practitioner corresponds interestingly to the work of those who teach very young children in negotiating purposes and meaning with children, and in supporting and extending their learning by all the means available. The technique is remarkably similar (see, for instance, the lines of approach to young children's linguistic development outlined by Wells, 1987). It suggests that the kind of research envisaged here would be readily acceptable and relatively easy to learn where researchers, whether practitioners or 'outsiders', could draw on experience of early childhood education.

Making classroom changes

Elliott and MacDonald (1975) say that new ideas must lead to actual changes if they are to be fully explored; they must be linked with action in the classroom so that they may be understood by being put into practice. This would mean both parties engaging in new and different practices so that they can evaluate the results. The second stage of this kind of research is, therefore, concerned with working together to implement developments agreed on in advance. The purpose is to see whether these developments would bring about the desired change and what their implications in terms of the underlying rationale might be for the practitioner's approach to the curriculum.

The benefits of collaborative research

There are many kinds of research in which staff collaboration might be sought, but the most fruitful kind for this approach must be the study of the effects of a change in provision for a specific group of children. With a study of this kind, the staff would be more closely involved. In a study of the way in which changes in provision affected the behaviour of a group of children, the evidence would need to be drawn from minute observations of behaviour, which would be compared on a before-and-after basis. There would be rich opportunities for the practitioner's professional development through growth in the capacity for awareness of the classroom and in the experience of evaluating work. For the researcher, there would be the unique opportunity to share in the insights and knowledge of someone who was an expert in relation to the particular group of children in question.

Conclusion

Many practitioners have a deep understanding of the potential role of high-quality early childhood education within the whole education system. They have already begun to consider what lines of further development we should be looking for. One of the most fruitful lines is that of action-research. The *Principles into Practice* project (Blenkin *et al.*, 1995) has researched and tried out strategies for professional development in which practitioners investigate their own settings. These strategies are both professionally enhancing and empowering (Kelly and Rose, 1996).

Discussion of the issues that arise in this way may indeed lead to changes in professional thinking and practice. Most of all, they are likely to give practitioners the added confidence they need to confront the challenges of the coming century:

- How can we ensure that all forms of preschool provision are well-supported and practitioners appropriately trained?
- Has the role of nursery schools, centres and classes, the holders of the tradition of British nursery education, changed substantially over the past few years? What future may they have in the light of recent educational developments?
- What light does the nursery curriculum shed on our general understanding of the curriculum, and of learning at other stages?

- How can equality of educational opportunity be ensured for the under-fives?
- How can action research contribute to the development of a better educational start for all under-eights?
- What should intending practitioners be given in the way of training and education? What is the role of child development in this?
- How can we best provide for children of nursery age in our present social and economic climate?
- What are the needs of parents in relation to preschool education? How can we best meet them?

Each of these questions brings challenges, and the hope that we may, by meeting these challenges, improve the education of our young children. Each of these questions leads on to the one central question: when, and how, are we going to give the developmental curriculum in this foundation stage of education the priority it deserves? The *Quality in Diversity* project has shown the commitment of practitioners to developmental approaches (Hurst, Burgess-Macy and Ouvry, 1996). We must hope that the coming years give them the opportunity to build on this commitment.

Further reading

Cox, T. (ed.) (1996) *The National Curriculum and the Early Years: Challenges and Opportunities*, Falmer Press, London.
Drummond, M. J. (1996) Whatever Next? Future Trends in Early Years Education in D. Whitebread (ed.) *Teaching and Learning in the Early Years*, Routledge, London.
Moss, P. and Penn, H. (1996) *Transforming Nursery Education*, Paul Chapman, London.

For discussion

Many early years issues tantalize us as we pass through the period of adjustment to radical educational reform. Cox (1996) asks whether the early years themselves should be redefined, and what are the years that should be considered those of the greatest developmental vulnerability. He decides in favour of the age-phase birth to eight, within which birth to three, three to five and five to eight are distinct phases, but this then raises the question of how we distinguish and safeguard the education and care needs of the children in these phases. Has not the admission of four-year-olds to reception classes cast doubt on our ability to do this?

Moss and Penn (1996) believe that the whole nature of nursery education will have to change and that its curriculum is neither a good foundation for children nor appropriate to the needs of parents as educators; yet the apparent complexity of the nursery curriculum is largely due to the priority that it gives to children's individual development and their learning at home. Is a developmental curriculum really such a difficult proposition to understand?

Drummond (1996) encourages us to think about the language in which we express our aims for children: 'Starting "where the child is", for all its familiarity as a slogan, as an "educational desideratum", is simply not the best place to start; it is simply not the best way of conceptualising the enterprise of early years education' (p. 339). If we agree that 'starting where the child is' is not an adequate way of conveying how we try to educate young children, what should we put in its place? Drummond suggests that we should pay more attention to the powers that children have, 'their powers to do, to think, to feel, to know and understand, to represent and express.' (ibid, p.339) She discusses the New Zealand curriculum based on this approach, and leads us to think about how we can provide a curriculum which embodies our intentions and hopes for children's powers to do, to feel, to think, to know and understand and to represent and express. All too often, these powers are diminished by education. How can our actions ensure that, instead, they are expanded and enhanced?

References

Abrahams, E. (1989) I had this other life, in Jewish Women in London Group, *Generations of Memories*, The Women's Press, London.

Athey, C. (1990) *Extending Thought in Young Children*, Paul Chapman, London.

Atkin, J., Bastiani, J. and Goode, J. (1988) *Listening to Parents*, Croom Helm, London.

Barrett, G. (1986) *Starting School: an Evaluation of the Experience*, AMMA, Norwich.

Bennett, N., Wood, L. and Rogers, S. (1997) *Teaching Through Play: Teachers' thinking and classroom practice*, Open University Press, Buckingham.

Bettelheim, B. (1975) *The Uses of Enchantment*, Thames and Hudson, London.

Blenkin, G. and Kelly, A. V. (1981) *The Primary Curriculum*, Paul Chapman, London.

Blenkin, G. M. and Kelly, A. V. (eds.) (1996) *Early Childhood Education: A Developmental Curriculum* (2nd edn) Paul Chapman, London.

Blenkin, G. M. and Kelly, A. V. (eds.) (1994) *The National Curriculum and Early Learning*, Paul Chapman, London.

Blenkin, G. M., Hurst, V., Whitehead, M. R. and Yue, N. Y. L. (1995) *Principles into Practice: Improving the Quality of Children's Early Learning. Phase One Report*, Goldsmiths' College, University of London.

Blenkin, G. M. and Whitehead, M. (1996) Creating a context for development, in G. M. Blenkin and A. V. Kelly (eds.) op. cit.

Blyth, W. A. L. (1984) *Development, Experience and Curriculum in Primary Education*, Croom Helm, London.

Board of Education (1931) *Primary Education* (the Hadow Report), HMSO, London.

Bredekamp, S. (ed.) (1987) *Developmentally Appropriate Practice in Programs Serving Children From Birth Through Age 8*, National Association for the Education of Young Children (NAEYC), Washington DC.

Bruce, T. (1987) *Early Childhood Education*, Hodder & Stoughton, Sevenoaks.

Bruce, T. (1991) *Time to Play in Early Childhood Education*, Hodder and Stoughton, London.

Bruner, J. (ed.) (1975) *Play: Its Role in Development and Education*, Penguin Books, Harmondsworth.

Bruner, J. (1980) *Under Five in Britain*, Grant McIntyre, London.

Bruner, J. (1984) *In Search of Mind*, Harper Colophon, New York.

Bruner, J. and Haste, H. (eds.) (1987) *Making Sense: Young Children Construct the World*, Methuen, London.

Butler, D. (1988) *Babies Need Books*, Penguin Books, London.

Carnegie Corporation (1994) *Starting Points: Meeting the Needs of our Youngest Children*, Carnegie Corporation, New York.

Central Advisory Council for Education (1963) *Half Our Future* (the Newsom Report), HMSO, London.

Central Advisory Council for Education (1967) *Children and their Primary Schools* (the Plowden Report), HMSO, London.

Clark, M. (ed.) (1987) *Roles, Responsibilities and Relationships in the Education of the Young Child*, University of Birmingham.

Clark, M. (1988) *Children Under Five: Educational Research and Evidence*, Gordon and Breach, London.

Cleave, S. and Brown, S. (1989) *Four Year Olds in School*, NFER, Windsor.

Cleave, S., Jowett, S. and Bate, M. (1982) *And So To School*, NFER/Nelson, Windsor.

Coltman, P. and Whitebread, D. (1996) My Mum would pay anything for chocolate cake! Organising the whole curriculum: enterprise projects in the early years, in D. Whitebread (ed.) *Teaching and Learning in the Early Years*, Routledge, London.

Cousins, J. (1990) Are your little Humpty Dumpties floating or sinking?, *Early Years*, Vol. 10, no. 2, pp. 28–38.

Cox, T. (ed.) (1996) *The National Curriculum and the Early Years: Challenges and Opportunities*, Falmer Press, London.

David, T. (1990) *Under Five – Under Educated?* Open University Press, Milton Keynes.

Department of Education and Science (1989a) *Statistical Bulletin*, HMSO, London.

Department of Education and Science (1989b) *International Statistical Comparisons of the Participation in Education and Day Care of Three to Six Year Olds*, HMSO, London.

Department of Education and Science (1989c) *The Education of Children Under Five*, HMSO, London.

Department of Health (1990) *Registration of Day Care Facilities*, Consultation paper no. 14, HMSO, London.

Donaldson, M. (ed.) (1978) *Children's Minds*, Fontana/Collins, Glasgow.

Dowling, M. (1988) *Education 3 to 5*, Paul Chapman, London.

Drummond, M. J. (1993) *Assessing Children's Learning*, David Fulton, London.

Drummond, M. J. (1996) Whatever Next? Future Trends in Early Years Education in D. Whitebread (ed.) op. cit.

Dunn, J. (1988) *The Beginnings of Social Understanding*, Blackwell, Oxford.

Early Childhood Education Forum (1997, draft papers) *Quality in Diversity in Early Learning: a framework for early childhood practitioners*, National Children's Bureau, London.

Early Years Curriculum Group (1989) *Early Childhood Education: the Early Years Curriculum and the National Curriculum*, Trentham Books, Stoke-on-Trent.

Early Years Curriculum Group (1992) *First Things First: Educating Young Children*, Madeleine Lindley, Oldham.

Early Years Curriculum Group (forthcoming 1998) *Interpreting the National Curriculum*, Open University Press, Buckingham.

Edgington, M. (forthcoming, 1998) *The Nursery Teacher in Action* (2nd edn), Paul Chapman, London.

Egan, K. (1988) *Primary Understanding*, Routledge, New York.

Eisner, E. (1996) *Cognition and Curriculum reconsidered*, (2nd edn) Paul Chapman, London.

Elliott, J. and MacDonald, B. (1975) *People in Classrooms*, Centre for Applied Research, University of East Anglia, Norwich.

Elliott, J., Bridges, D., Elliott, D., Gibson, R. and Nias, J. (1981) *School Accountability*, Grant McIntyre, London.

Fawcett, M. (1996) *Learning Through Child Observation*, Jessica Kingsley Publishers, London.

Fisher, H. A. L. (1918) quoted in *The Times*, 14.3.97, 'The Children's Charter'.

Fisher, J. (1996) *Starting from the Child*, Open University Press, Buckingham.

Goldschmied, E. (1989) Play and Learning in the First Year of Life, in V. Williams (ed.) op. cit.

Goldschmied, E. (1993) *Infants at Work*, National Children's Bureau, London.

Goldschmied, E. with Anita Hughes (1992) *Heuristic Play: Children of 12–20 months exploring everyday objects*, National Children's Bureau, London.

Goldschmied, E. and Jackson, S. (1994) *People Under Three: Young Children in Day Care*, Routledge, London.

Goldschmied, E. and Selleck, D. (1996) *Communication Between Babies in their First Year*, National Children's Bureau, London.

Graham, J. (1995) *The Garden*, Trustees of the Science Museum, London.

Guha, M. (1996) Play in School, in G. Blenkin and A. V. Kelly (eds.) op. cit.

Gura, P. (ed.) (1992) *Exploring Learning: Young Children and Blockplay*, Paul Chapman, London.

Hannon, P. and James, S. (1990) Parents' and teachers' perspectives on preschool literacy development, *British Educational Research Journal*, Vol. 16, no. 3, pp. 259–72.

Harris, P. (1990) Quoted in *Oxford Today*, Vol. 2, no. 2, pp. 18–19.

House of Commons Education, Science and Arts Committee (1988/1989) *Educational Provision for the Under Fives*, HMSO, London.

Hughes, M. (1983) Teaching arithmetic to preschool children, *Educational Review*, Vol. 35, no. 2, pp. 162–73.

Hurst, V. (1988) Parents and Professionals: Partnership in Early Childhood Education, in G. Blenkin and A. V. Kelly (eds.) op. cit.

Hurst, V. Burgess-Macey, C. and Ouvry, M. (1997) Who decides the meaning of 'quality' in early childhood education? in *Early Education*, no. 21, January.

Hutchin, V. (1996) *Tracking Significant Achievement in the Early Years*, Hodder and Stoughton, London.

Hutchins, P. (1968) *Rosie's Walk*, Bodley Head, London.

Isaacs, S. (1929) *The Nursery Years* (1971 reprint), Routledge & Kegan Paul, London.

Isaacs, S. (1930) *Intellectual Growth in Young Children*, Routledge & Kegan Paul, London.

Isaacs, S. (1933) *Social Development in Young Children*, Routledge & Kegan Paul, London.

Kelly, A. V. (1986) *Knowledge and Curriculum Planning*, Paul Chapman, London.

Kelly, A. V. (1990) *The National Curriculum: A Critical Review*, Paul Chapman, London.

Kelly, A.V. and Rose, J. (1996) Action Research and the early years of education, *Early Years*, Vol. 17, no. 1, pp. 41–6.

Lawrence, D. H. (1915) *The Rainbow* (edited by M. Kinkead-Weekes, 1989), Cambridge University Press.

Matthews, J. (1994) *Helping Young Children to Draw and Paint*, Hodder and Stoughton, London.

Merttens, R. and Vass, J. (1990a) Assessing the nation: blueprints without tools, *Primary Teaching Studies*, Vol. 5, no. 3, June, pp. 222–39.

Merttens, R. and Vass, J. (1990b) *IMPACT – Sharing Maths Culture*, Falmer Press, Lewes.

Moss, P. and Penn, H. (1996) *Transforming Nursery Education*, Paul Chapman, London.

National Foundation for Educational Research/Schools Curriculum Development Council (1987) *Four Year Olds in School*, NFER, Windsor.

Newson, J. and E. (1977) *Perspectives on School at Seven Years Old*, Allen & Unwin, London.

Osborn, A. F. and Milbank, J. E. (1987) *The Effects of Early Education*, Clarendon Press, Oxford.

Pascal, C. and Ghaye, A. (1988) *Four Year Old Children in Reception Classrooms*, Worcester College of Higher Education.

Piaget, J. (1973) *The Child's Conception of the World*, Granada, London.

Pilling, D. and National Children's Bureau (1990) *Escape from Disadvantage*, Falmer Press, Lewes.

Public Attitude Surveys (1989) *Parental Awareness of School Education*, DES, London.

Pugh, G., De'Ath, E. and Smith, C. (1994) *Confident Parents, Confident Children*, National Children's Bureau, London.

Pugh, G. and De'Ath, E. (1996) *The Needs of Parents: Practice and Policy in Parent Education*, Macmillan Education, London.

Rachel McMillan Nursery School (1988) *A Curriculum Document*, Rachel McMillan Nursery School, McMillan Street, London SE8.

Robert Owen Nursery School (1989) *Robert Owen Writing Book*, Robert Owen Nursery School, Conley Street, London SE10.

Robson, S. (1996) The physical environment, in S. Robson and S. Smedley (eds.) op. cit.

Robson, S. and Smedley, S. (eds.) (1996) *Education in Early Childhood: First Things First*, David Fulton in association with the Roehampton Institute, London.

School Curriculum and Assessment Authority (1996) *Desirable Outcomes for Children's Learning on Entering Compulsory Education*, SCAA, London.

School Curriculum and Assessment Authority (1997) *The National Framework for Baseline Assessment: Criteria and procedures for the accreditation of Baseline Assessment Schemes*, SCAA, London.

Sestini, E. (1987) The quality of learning and experiences for four year olds in nursery and infant classes, in NFER/SCDC, op. cit.

Siraj-Blatchford, I. (1994) *The Early Years: Laying the Foundations for Racial Equality*, Trentham Books, Stoke-on-Trent.

Smith, P. K. (1988) Children's play and its role in early development, in A. D. Pellegrini (ed.) *Psychological Bases for Early Education*, Wiley, Chichester.

Smith, T. (1980) *Parents and Preschool*, Grant McIntyre, London.

Spodek, B. (1982) *Handbook of Research in Early Education*, The Free Press/ Macmillan, New York.

Sponseller, D. (1982) Play and early education, in B. Spodek (ed.) op. cit.

Stenhouse, L. (1975) *An Introduction to Curriculum Research and Development*, Heinemann, London.

Task Group on Assessment and Testing (1987) *A Report*, Department of Education and Science, London.

Tizard, B. and Hughes, M. (1984) *Young Children Learning: Talking and Thinking at Home and at School*, Fontana, London.

Tizard, B., Blatchford, P., Burke, J., Farquhar, C. and Plewis, L. (1988) *Young Children at School in the Inner City*, Lawrence Erlbaum, London.

Towill, E. (1997) The Constructive Use of Role Play at Key Stage 3, *Teaching History*, no. 86, January.

Trevarthen, C. (1993) Conversations with the Infant Communicator, *Winnicott Papers*, Squiggle Foundation, London.

Trevarthen, C. (1996) First contracts of mutual understanding, Goldsmiths' Association for Early Childhood Conference Report, 1996, Goldsmiths' College, London.

Vygotsky, L. S. (1966) Play and its role in the mental development of the child, *Soviet Psychology*, Vol. 12, no. 6, pp. 62–76 (quoted in J. Bruner (ed.) 1975, op. cit.).

Vygotsky, L. S. (1978) *Mind in Society*, Harvard University Press, Cambridge, Mass.

Watt, J. (1987) Continuity in early education, in M. Clark (ed.) op. cit.

Wells, G. (1983) Talking with children, in M. Donaldson, R. Grieve, and C. Pratt (eds.) op. cit.

Wells, G. (1985) *Language, Learning and Education*, NFER/Nelson, Windsor.

Wells, G. (1987) *The Meaning Makers*, Hodder & Stoughton, Sevenoaks.

Whitebread, D. (ed.) (1996) *Teaching and Learning in the Early Years*, Routledge, London.

Whitehead, M. (1990) *Language and Literacy in the Early Years* 2nd edn (1997), Paul Chapman, London.

Wood, D. (1988) *How Children Think and Learn*, Blackwell, Oxford.

Woodhead, M. (1986) When should children go to school?, *Primary Education Review*, no. 25, Spring, pp. 10–14.

Woodhead, M. (1989) School starts at five . . . or four years old?, *Journal of Education Policy*, Vol. 4, no. 1, pp. 1–21.

Index